WOMEN OF INDIA

WOMEN OF INDIA

By

Otto Rothfeld

GYAN

Published by

Gyan Publishing House
5, Ansari Road
Daryaganj, New Delhi-110002
Phone: 011-47034999, 9811692060
E-mail: books@gyanbooks.com

Distribution Network
gyanbooks.com
India, USA, Canada, UK, Australia, France

ISBN : 978-81-212-6510-2 (PB)
First Published, 1920

2nd Impression 2022

Printed at: Gyan Press, Delhi.

WOMEN OF INDIA
Author: Otto Rothfeld

WOMEN OF INDIA

BY

OTTO ROTHFELD, F.R.G.S., I.C.S.

AUTHOR OF

'INDIAN DUST,' 'LIFE AND ITS PUPPETS'

'WITH PEN AND RIFLE IN KISHTWAR'

ILLUSTRATED BY

M. V. DHURANDHAR

DEDICATED

WITH THE DEVOTION OF A LIFETIME

TO THE KINDEST OF FRIENDS

MRS ARGYLL ROBERTSON

A CONSTANT WELL-WISHER OF

INDIAN WOMANHOOD

Contents

List of Illustrations

As they are

"Oh hail! O bright great God, in the form of that brown-eyed beautiful thing before me, that fills me with astonishment and laughter and supreme delight."

A Draught of the Blue. PROFESSOR BAIN.

Chapter I

AS THEY ARE

OTHERS had written even before Vatsyana the Wise wrote his "Gospel of Love." At that time the power of the Yávans and the Sákas was outstretched over the land. They were peoples that had come out of Persia and Bactria and obscure Scythia, many of them men with the blood of those Ionian soldiers who had marched with Alexander and settled with Eastern wives under Eastern skies. The teachings of Gautama, the Indian prince, they had made their own; and to the countries in which they ruled they had brought the peace of Buddha and the temperate fruitions of Greece. On all the great trade-routes were monasteries of Buddhist monks and large caravanserais for merchants and pilgrims. Even as far as the sands of Lopnor, far across the roof of the world, and to the Gobi desert, where the Chinese land begins, the tribes that gave rulers to India had set their posts and planted their colonies. On cunningly-sealed wedges of wood they sent their royal orders to the wardens of their frontiers and on palm-leaves from the Indian coasts they inscribed the lore that gave the illumination of God to settlements on the mountains and in the Central Asian deserts. In the shrines or stupas that they raised to Buddha, the wise teacher, they had dadoes and frescoes painted in tempera by some Titianus or Heliodorus from the Hellenized Levant, adventurers of a fine Grecian courage, who scattered their harmonious energies and their joy in life over the Indian world. Along the trade-routes marched merchants' caravans, burdened with silks and rare spices, that found their way from China to the Black Sea or the precarious ports on the Arabian Coast.

"Women," wrote the professors of love, in that time of peace and enjoyment, "can be divided into four classes. There is she who is a pure lotus, and she who is fair as a picture, she whom they call hag and witch, and she who can be likened only to the female of the elephant." Of her who is as a lotus they wrote: "Her face is pleasant, like the full moon: her plump body is tender as the mustard flower: her skin is fine and soft as the golden lotus, fair and undarkened. Bright and beautiful are her eyes like those of the antelope, clear-cut and healthful. Her breast is firm and full and uplifted, and her neck shapely: her nose is straight and delightful. The scent of her body is like a lily newly burst. She walks delicately like a swan and her voice is low and musical as the note of the cuckoo, calling softly in the summer day. She is clothed in clean white garments and she delights in rich jewels and adornments. She is gracious and clever, pious and respectful, a lover of God, a listener to the virtuous and the wise."

As they are

Of the manner of living of a virtuous woman it is further written by Vatsyana the Wise: "A virtuous woman that hath affection to her husband shall in all things act according to his wishes as if he were divine. She shall keep the house well-cleansed and arrange flowers of every kind in the different chambers and surround the house with a garden and make the floor smooth and polished, so that all things be meet and seemly. Above all she shall venerate the shrine of the Household Deities. To the parents of her husband she shall behave as is meet and proper, speaking to them in few words and softly, not laughing loud in their presence, but being always quiet and respectful without self-will and contradiction. She shall always consider in the kitchen what her husband likes and dislikes and shall seek to please him. Always she will sit down after him and rise before him: and when she hears his footsteps as he returns home, she will get up and meet him and do aught that he desires. If her husband do wrong, she shall not unduly reproach him, but show him a slight displeasure and rebuke him in words of fondness and affection. And when she goes to her husband when they are alone, she will wear bright coloured garments and many jewels and anklets and will perfume herself with sweet ointments and in her hair place flowers."

Many generations have passed and other races—Hunas and Gujjars and Mongols—have invaded India. And asceticism has squeezed the people in its dry hand, and there has been war and bigotry and pestilence. Yet even now the teachings are not quite forgotten. Many a one there still is among the women of India, of whom it can with truth be said: "She is even as a golden lotus."

Now, again, the sovereigns of India rule over many regions and send their royal messages to the uttermost ends of the earth. Again the great trade-routes pass through India and the merchandise of East and of West meet in the harbours of Bombay and Calcutta. Castes and peoples feel their way to a common nationality and a fresher spirit, and before their eyes breaks the morning light of a new Renaissance. And in the women of new India the old texts revive to a more vigorous flesh and spirit.

Stand of an evening on the Queen's Road in Bombay, looking over the wide curve of Back Bay, where the lights of the city fade away into the distances of the sea and on the right the hill throws its contour against the darkening sky. They pass here, brightly-clad, quietly smiling, modestly distant, the women of India at their newest and most modern, yet in essentials formed by the ancient rule. They are discarding perhaps the habits of dark ages of misrule and superstition, but they cling none the less to the spirit of old India—to those principles hallowed at its best and freshest age. In their cars the wives and children of rich merchants glide through the crowd. On the back seat, in the shadow of the cabriolet top, a glimpse of gold-brocade can be caught

A PATHARE PRABHU

or the tone of a fair brown skin. Here a Bhatia lady passes, come originally from the hot plains of the Cutch Peninsula, the wife of a millionaire cotton-spinner or a financial agent. Or there, in gracefully-draped mantle[1] and Paris-made shoes and stockings, a Saraswat Brahman lady or a Pathare Prabhu, with that lustrous pallor that is brought by the warm breezes from the sea, goes on her way to her club to play tennis or drink afternoon tea. Seated in open carriages or strolling along the pavement to taste the freshness of the sea-breeze, are hundreds of Parsi girls, in dresses of every hue, with the heavy velvet borders that they affect, gossiping, nodding to their friends, laughing and chattering. Poorer women dart across the street, pulling children after them through the busy traffic, and carrying their youngest on their hip astride. A sweeper woman brushes fallen leaves into the gutter. Through all the noise of motors and of the trains that dash along the disfiguring railway, the sound of a bell clanged at the temple door by a worshipper may be heard and, at sunset, the call to prayer from the minaret of a mosque. Behind a high wall, half-way down the fashionable drive, a red light rises against the darkness from the flames which consume the city's dead.

Chiefly the notes that strike are of nature and sex. These women are so thoroughly women, beyond and

[1] The *sari* has throughout this book been rendered by the English word "mantle," though as an equivalent it is misleading. For a description of the *sari* as it is, see Chapter VIII.

above all else. Except perhaps among the Parsis, where English customs have been sometimes too closely copied, there is no trace of the beings, women in age, but stunted and warped and with the ignorance of children, that, seen in other countries, create an uneasiness as at the touch of something unnatural and perverse. Here are the clear brows and smiling faces of those who *know*, to whom sex is a necessary part of life, and motherhood a pride and duty. They dress and adorn themselves, because they are women, with a husband to please and to govern. Their sex is frank and admitted: as women they know their place in the world and as women they seek a retiring modesty. Their very aloofness, their seclusion, gives them half their charm: and they know it. Not for them, for instance, the dismal methods of American schools, where mixed classes and a common play-ground rub away all the attraction of the sexes and make their growing pupils dully kin like brother and sister. In India women are so much valued and attain half their power because they are only occasionally seen and seldom met. It is the rarest flowers that are sought at the peril of life itself. It is for the women who live veiled and separated that men crave, captives of passion at a first quick-taken glance. A wife who is not the familiar companion of every walk or game, who is never seen through the long business hours—with what delight the husband, unjaded by the constant sight of women in street or office, seeks her at last in the

WATER-CARRIER FROM AHMEDABAD

inner apartments where she waits with smiles and flowers!

How natural they are—true, that is, to the natural instincts and purposes of women, not without womanly artifice—is most apparent from a contrast. Their shyness, even their self-consciousness with men, is of a woman's nature. Their love of jewelry, their little tricks of manner, why, the very way they stand are, after all, the natural derivatives of womanhood. Of motherhood they have no shame: they celebrate marriage and childbirth frankly with a fine candour. Their garments drape them in soft flowing lines falling in downward folds over the rounded contours of the body—draperies full of grace and restful. In Europe women still adhere to a deformity brought in by German barbarism in the dark ages. With curious appliances, they distort and misshape the middle of their bodies from quite early childhood till—the negation of all beauty—in place of a natural human figure appear two disjunct parts joined, as it were, mechanically by a tightened horizontal band. From their passive acceptance of routine, women will bear traditional deformity, in spite of illness and the constant weariness of nervous disorders. What is difficult to understand is that—with all their wish to please—they can endure its patent ugliness. Pleasing is the contrast of the Indian mantle, gracefully draped over head and shoulders and falling in vertical folds to the feet, and of the gaily-stitched and neat little fitting bodice of the

Hindu lady. Her head with its smooth hair, decked with simple gold ornaments or fresh flowers, half covered by the silken veil, is well poised and beautiful. She poses on it no twisted straws, dyed in metallic colours, no fantastic covering, hung with pieces of dead bird.

The step of the Indian woman walking is a thing of joy. It has in it nothing of the mincing awkward shuffle or of the disgracious manly stride. But at her best see her walking in the country villages, where her frame is trained to a graceful poise by the constant carriage of water-pots balanced on her head as she steps unshod down the dusty lanes or the sloping banks of the river.

In the villages, indeed, it is round the well that woman's life circles. Where the dry plains stretch away westward from Ahmedabad over land cast back by the sea, the walls of mud-built villages stand square against the blank horizon, where they were raised against the raids of Kathi or of Koli freebooters. Here in the hot spring months from March to July, before the grey rains turn the land to a sticky swamp, the sun from dawn to its setting beats savagely on the sand. In these little townships, high-walled, with iron-studded gates, the women have to seek the well early. An hour before the day, before even the false dawn throws its silver flicker over the sky, they come from every quarter to the one great well which supplies the place. Oh! the early morning chatter which wakes one from his sleep! Ropes

SWEEPER

and buckets splash upon the water and pot rings against brass pot. They come in scores, of every caste and age, merchants' wives and pretty *noblesse*, cultivators and labourers, old women, widows and mothers, and little naked children—how frail and tender their lines!—hardly able to stagger homewards under the load. With hurried prattle they talk of the night and the coming day, of the prices of the bazaar and the scandal of a wanton neighbour or the coming visit of a priest. The day dawns and the full white orb of the sun, white living heat like molten metal, rises suddenly into the level sky. The women finish drawing water as best they can and turn home. They walk straight, those women, two copper pots balancing easily on the head, another large pitcher lightly held against the hip, easily moving as they talk and smile. No wonder if a young man, idly, may sometimes stroll towards the well. For some there are who looking on these women of Káthiawád passing, with golden skins and full oval faces, must say to themselves, as said Solomon, "How fair and how pleasant art thou, O love, for delights: this thy stature is like to a palm-tree and thy breasts to clusters of grapes."

Next to the well, it is at the temple that the life of a woman centres. For her every thought and act is moulded from childhood to the day of death by the present reality of religion. Her childhood is an adoration, marriage a sacrament, wifehood an oblation: in motherhood she finds at once sacrifice and worship: while life and death alike are a quest and a resignation. Life, as to herself she interprets it, is not so much action as a response to divine ordinance, receptive and submissive. She awaits love and may yield to joy: but she expects them as a handmaiden, humbly, without striving and without insistence. And the daily ritual in which her life of service finds its symbol is the scattering of flowers upon the images of God, the singing of His praises, and the circumambulation of His sacred shrine. At the temple she makes her humble vows, for a husband's kindness or the supreme gift of childbirth. And there, from the fulness of her heart, she pours out thanksgiving for the blessings of her state. And if at the end perhaps she die childless and a widow, it is not singular if she leave her wealth to the further endowment of the temple and the greater glory of God Rama and his Sita, the divine pair of her worship.

The heroism of Indian womanhood has found its loftiest expression in the Rajput nobility, with the great Queens who have fought and been slain in battle or self-immolated on the funeral pyre: its piety is a transfiguration in the Brahman and the merchant class: and woman's love with its transcendent ecstasy burns like a glowing ember on the hearth of every soul. But for devotion to labour, uninspired by any ideal other than its mere fulfilment, one turns to the menial castes that, from century to century, have lived closest to their own soil. Thus on the stony uplands of the Deccan, the women of the untouchable Mahars—descended probably from some once ruling race, long tragically overthrown—labour without respite in the hard fields at their husbands' sides. But, furthermore, they bear and suckle children, cook the family food and do the work of their poor household. Ceaseless labour it is, done without bitterness, in a humble resignation. A rough life, yet not without redemption! Their hardships are recognized and their pleasures shared: they stand side by side with their menfolk, comrades by their service. They hold themselves upright, not without the pride of service, and to the eye that comprehends, they have even a rough attraction, like a picture by Millet, in their sturdy strength, earthy and fruitful.

The book of Indian womanhood has many pages, and each page is different, one from the other. Living in a wide continent, the speech of one group of women is not as the speech of another. And in faith they are not one, nor in blood nor habit. But though the leaves of the book are of various type, yet they are all of one shape, bound in one cloth and colour. For to all of them, above all else, is contentment with their own womanhood, faith in religion and the natural hope of love. An unremitting devotion and an unfailing tenderness, that is the Indian woman's service in the world; and it is her loving service that has given its best to the land. India has had great preachers and great thinkers, it has had and has brave soldiers. But more than the men, more even than their best and bravest, it is the women who have deserved well of the country. What they have won is the respect with which all men behave to stranger women. It is a rule of Indian manners that they should pass unnoticed and unremarked, even in the household of a friend, and, except perhaps among the lowest ruffians, there is none who would offend the modesty of a woman even by a gesture or an unseemly recognition. They can pass in the midst of crowds, as nurses pass in the most evil back-streets, without molestation or insult. For the women of India have raised an ideal, lofty and selfless, for all to behold: and they have come near its attainment. And with all its self-sacrifice and abnegation, with all its unremitting service, the ideal is not inhuman nor is it alien to the nature of womankind. It allows for weaknesses, it is kind to faults, and it aspires frankly to the joys of a fulfilment deserved by service. Not without reason did the writers of old India liken the perfect woman of their land to a lotus, in that she "is tender as a flower."

Marriage in India

"Thilke blissful lyf
That is betwixe an housband and his wyf:
And for to live under that holy bond
With which that first God man and womman bond.
'Non other lyf,' sayde he, 'is worth a bene:
For wedlock is so esy and so clene,
That in this world it is a paradys.'"

Marchantes Tale. CHAUCER.

Chapter II

MARRIAGE IN INDIA

In all countries, for a woman marriage has a significance not only greater than but different in quality from the significance it has for a man. It is not merely that to the man marriage is only one incident, however far-reaching in its effects and values, among the recurrent vicissitudes of life ; while to the woman, even if it be so regarded, it is at least the most conclusive of all incidents—that from which depends not alone her own comfort but rather the fulfilment of her whole being and function. A man's life is made up of the intermittent pursuit of many a quarry at the impulse of divergent passions, projected from time to time in varying light upon the evenly-moving background of the sub-conscious activities. He studies and his soul is engrossed in the niceties of the arts or the subtleties of philosophy. He finds satisfaction for his intellect and even his emotions in the choice of the fitting phrase for a description. At another time he rushes to sport, and, for many hours in the day and many days in the month, finds pleasant fatigue and final occupation in stalking the stag through the forest with its dry crackling leaves. In administration he makes a career : and he may be busy day and night with problems of finance, the just use of authority or the thousand questions of policy in a developing civilization. Whatever his profession may be, his work engages the greater portion of his life and all his highest and most useful energies. A man's pulse quickens its beat rapidly, and as easily falls again to a slow extreme of indolence and indifference. He does his best and finest work in the hours of rapid energy. It is then that he fulfils those functions of creation and fruitful activity which appertain to the male in the self-ordered organization of the world. But among those his union with his mate is not the most important. Rather it may be called the expenditure of a superfluous energy. He needs his mate only in the moments of excited passion, when his energies, unexhausted by duties that he counts more valuable, are at their strongest. But as a companion he values the woman that is given to him mainly in the hours of repose and leisure—those periods when the over-stimulated mind and body sink to the level of an indolent passivity. Companionship he seeks that his surroundings should be easy and congenial, when his work is done and he is weary. Again, when a man marries, he either has loved or will love other women and he knows in his heart that the wife, who is to share and make his home, can be only one, though perhaps the tenderest and sweetest, of his loving memories. Herein, for the woman who gives him her love, is the irony. Only with the man to whom all love is ashes and who can never kindle the fierce flame of passion, can she expect the sole and exclusive possession to which she is inclined by her own nature. From the

FISHER WOMAN OF SIND

man who can promise her his only love, the gift is of little value and his love but the thin shadow of a spectre. But she knows the man whose love is as a robe of purple or a diadem of rubies cannot be for her alone, wholly hers.

To the woman, however, marriage is the incident of all incidents, that one action to which all else in life—even the birth of her first male-child—is subsidiary and subordinate. She goes to her mate, in shyness and modesty, as to one who for the first time shall make her truly woman. At his touch the whole world changes and the very birds and flowers, the seas, the stars, and the heaven above, put on a different colour and murmur a new music. In a moment the very constitution of her body alters and her limbs take nobler curves and her figure blooms to a new splendour. Her mind and emotions grow: and the dark places which she had feared are seen to be sun-lit and lofty. Marriage is to her more than an incident, however revolutionary. It is rather the foundation of a new life, indeed a new life itself. For her, henceforth, her whole existence is but the one fact of being married. It is her career, her profession, her study, her joy, her everything. She lives no longer in herself but rather as her man's wife. "Half-body," the Sanscrit poets say, not untruly of the married woman.

In India, even more than in Europe, certainly more than in Northern Europe, marriage is to a woman everything. In early childhood she becomes aware, gradually and almost unconsciously, of the great central facts of nature. She lives in a household in which, along with the earning of daily bread, all talk freely of marriages and the birth of children. When a brother or sister is born, she is not excluded, and no one tells her tales of mysterious storks or cabbages. As she grows older, she hears the stories of Sita, the divine wife, and of Sakuntala, the loved princess: and the glowing winds of spring and the burning sun help to bring her to a quick maturity. Around her she sees her girl friends given in marriage to flower-crowned boy bridegrooms, brought on gold-caparisoned horses with beating of drums and bursting fire-works and much singing to the bridal bower and the sacred fire. She learns of widowhood and the life-long austerities imposed on a woman whose sin-haunted destiny drags her husband to the grave. In the household prayers she sees that her father needs her mother at his side for the due offering of oblations and the completion of the ritual. Of a woman unmarried, not a widow, she never hears and the very notion can hardly frame itself on the mirror of her mind. No wonder that, with her earliest reflections, she bends her thoughts upon the husband that is to come and to be her lord, to whom she will hold herself affianced by the will of God through all the moving cycle of innumerable deaths and existences.

Matrimony in India, in nearly every case, is stamped by one of two types, the marriage-contract of the Mussulmans, or the unions sanctified in the vast and extremely complex social system that is comprised under the general name of Hinduism. In theory, legally one might say, marriage among the Mussulmans of India is a contract that should in no way differ from that practised in other countries of Islam. A man and a woman bind themselves or are bound by a voidable contract which confers certain rights of maintenance and succession, in consideration of mutual comfort and cherishing. The contract, but not its sanction and consequences, can be repudiated at the man's will and, subject to certain intelligible limitations, at the claim of the woman. In all cases proper and ample provision is and must be made for the children. The woman who is divorced, or widowed, is in no way prevented from entering upon a fresh contract with another husband, rather she is encouraged and assisted so to do. Broadly speaking, this is the legal position in every Mussulman marriage. No other world-wide system has ever been so reasonable and so human. It is a legislation passed through the mouth of its Founder for all followers of the faith, as human beings bound in their relations to other men and women only by justice, which is the ultimate morality of the world. The interpretation of the Legislator's act has varied slightly in the jurisprudence of the "Four Pillars of the Faith," the talented authors of the four great law-schools of Islam. Among the Shiah sect in Persia, also, the rulings have been somewhat modified and extended in the judge-made law of the ecclesiastical courts: and contracts for temporary marriages—marriages limited to a stated, sometimes a short, period—have for example been recognized and ratified. But these are all variations which show the more clearly how, in essence, the matrimony of Islam is a thing of law, an agreement for certain purposes and with certain consequences, between human beings regarded in their capacity as agents in a very human world. That this should be so is, in fact, a necessary consequence from the whole character of Islam. For the very essence of Islam is its rationalism. God created the world that He might be *known*. From the children of Adam He expects praise and He exacts obedience and resignation. By His strength and will He divides among them their shares of blissful or unkind environment. But in the activities of human life, when they have satisfied the requirements of prostration to the All-Powerful Creator, He leaves them free to move as they will under the guidance of the highest human morality—justice. In the verses that are concerned with the relations between man and man, the Book of the Qor'an is as rational as the ethics of Aristotle or the commentary of a student. Even the Persian mystics, that were clad in wool, the children of the Tasawwuf—they who represent Indo-Aryan mysticism outcropping from the level calculations of the Semitic faith—sought, in the main, only to modify the attitude of man to God. In place of obedience, with its scale of service and reward, they set up a spiritual ecstasy of love, and in this love they hoped to unite the human consciousness with the divine thought of which it is a manifestation and in which it seeks absorption. But the way with its four stages of ascent, by which they pointed the road to final

MUSSULMAN ARTISAN FROM KÁTHIAWÁD

union with absolute Being, rarely traversed the ethics of human action in the phenomenal world. With the commands of justice and with the contracts which made possible and legitimate the companionship and love of man and woman they never really sought to interfere.

This then is the plan, clear, reasonable, and humane. But in the practice of India, it must be confessed, there have been many deviations. They live after all, the Mussulmans of India, among a population, of which they form but the seventh part, highly religious, mystical, seeing in all things magic and the supernatural. In great part they derive from the castes and tribes of Hindu India, converted to the creed by conquest, interest, or persuasion. Large sections still retain and are governed by the Hindu customary law of their former tribe. The rich Mussulman merchants of Bombay, who traverse the ocean like other Sindbads and seek their merchandise in the Eastern Archipelagoes or in the new colonies of the African continent, peaceful merchants of whom a large sect still perpetuates the doctrines of the Shaik of the Mountain and reveres the memory, without the practice, of the Assassins, follow in their domesticities and the laws of succession rules whose significance depends from the mystic teachings of the Hindu sages. In Gujarat the Mussulman nobility preserve with respect the names and practices of the Rajput chiefs from whom they are descended. They marry within families of cognate origin and transmit their estates and dignities by a rule that is widely apart from the jurisprudence of Islam. But that marriage is indefeasibly binding on a woman for all time, even after death's parting, so that the widowed wife may never seek another husband—these are ideas whose ultimate basis is a view of the world as a thing moved and deflected by magic and magical interpositions. Yet these opinions of the surrounding Hindu population have invaded the Mussulman household also. The proud families which claim direct descent from the Prophet of Arabia have in practice created an absolute prohibition of re-marriage. And in many families of temporal rank the same veto is observed, as having in it something exclusive and patrician. Even among the common people, it is only the first marriage which is known by the significant name of "gladness," while the corrector Arabic term has been degraded with a baser meaning to the marriage of a widow. In practice, too, the wise provisions of the law for dowries and the separate maintenance of a wife have been neglected, while divorce is much discountenanced and the claims of an ill-used or insufficiently-cherished wife to a decree are ignored or even forgotten. Child-marriage has become the rule, and consent to a life-long bond under a contract which has come to be regarded almost as inviolable, is only too often given on behalf of the young girl by a relation indifferent to all except wealth and position.

Yet such is the radiance, so purifying the chemistry of reason that, in spite of superstition, it continues to oxidize and revive the body which it permeates. The inroads of Mongol tribes from Central Asia—recent and bigoted converts—laid low the body politic of Islam. For five dark centuries Mussulman culture was turned into a wilderness. In India Islam has been further obscured, as has been shown, by the encroaching customs and feelings of peoples who conceived life on an incompatible and magical apprehension. Yet the word of rationalism was never wholly silent, and the thought of human justice in a world of causation persisted, however feebly, to sweeten and humanize the relations of men and women in the fundamental contract of matrimony. The Mussulman woman in her family wields great power and influence. She is consulted and made much of to an extent rare in most countries. The words of the Qor'an are a constant inspiration to her husband; and he knows himself to be bound to cherish as best he can the woman who is described in Scripture as a field which he should cultivate and as a partner to whom he owes kindness and protection. Under this inspiration he can hardly fail to estimate at its highest the value of womanhood; for even in heaven his promised reward includes the pleasures of beautiful and enchanting women. Thus has Omar Khayyam written in the 188th Rubaiyat:—

> "They say there will be a paradise and fair women and black-eyed virgins,
> And there, say they, will be pure wine and honey.
> So if we adore our wine and our beloved, why, 'tis lawful
> Since the end of all this business will be even thus."

The Mussulman religion idealizes above everything manliness and the manly virtues; and it certainly does not undervalue the place of sex in human life. Now, it is the virile man who yields most readily to the sway of woman. His very vigour impels him to her side: and in the reactions from enterprise and affairs he wishes to be soothed by her companionship and delight. So it is true that the Mussulman woman in India has seldom cause for complaint within her household. The day's labour done, husband and children gather in the inner apartments, where she rules, and devote themselves to her comfort and entertainment.

Where she suffers, if at all, is from the too rigid custom of the *purdah* or female seclusion. What in India distorted the modest injunction of the Prophet that women should veil their faces before strange men to the excessive and even fantastic *purdah* system, is a question still hotly debated by Indian reformers and publicists.

Hindus accuse the Mussulman population of introducing the system: Mussulmans point to the more rational habit of other Islamic countries and lay the charge to the door of the Rajput nobility. Whatever may have been the original cause, the results are sometimes ludicrous and injurious. Applied as it is in the houses of nobles and rich merchants, the custom is sufficiently tolerable and even advantageous. The ladies have gardens in which to exercise their limbs: they drive in screened carriages to see the town or enjoy the country breezes; they have liberty to visit at all hours the houses of their women friends and

PATHAN WOMAN

profit by their conversation. They have light and air and reasonable freedom. Like many other points of aristocratic ceremony, the practice of seclusion is valued largely by the inconvenience it causes to others. It needs little knowledge of feminine nature to appreciate the pleasurable sense of dignity it causes the wealthy *purdah* lady when, at a visit, she sees all male servants and even the owner of the house sent hurrying to hide in remote corners while she makes her stately progress from her carriage to her friends' apartments. On her travels she notes with pride the tumult in the crowded station when sheets are held across the platform to seclude her from stranger eyes as she slowly strolls to her compartment. But to apply the same etiquette to the middle and the poorer classes is little short of madness. Yet there are many parts of India, where the Mussulman population, and especially their womankind, insist with melancholy pride on these observances, whatever their poverty and decay. There are found in little crumbling mud-hovels, clinging to the base of ancient forts and palaces, women who spend their useless lives crouched in a dark ill-smelling room, where the light of day and the breath of energy and aspiration can never reach them. They bear feeble children: fall sick of a decline or internal ailments: and go out in premature senility like a candle in a choked tunnel. Fortunately the sturdy Mussulman peasantry of the north know nothing of these follies: nor in Káthiawád and Gujarát do the Mussulman artisans, who are here pictured, ruin their homes by this disastrous aping of an aristocracy. But even with this drawback—one maintained, it must be remembered, mainly by the same feminine lust for pride and precedence which in England keeps the clerk's wife from cooking a dinner—it is in general true that the rationalism of the system has produced mutual respect and affection, together with much courtesy and chivalry, between the sexes.

The Afghan or Pathan woman is in many ways apart from her Mussulman sister of the real India of the plains. Strong, virile, courageous, but treacherous and illiterate, the Afghan tribes are still narrowly within the pale of savagery. They are hillmen, living in secluded valleys or rocky fastnesses, with the virtues of their kind, but far removed from those urbane polities which in all languages and races have set the type of civilization. In Islam the word for civilization is as much derived from the word for "city," "Medinah," as in the languages that trace their descent from the Latins. Of gentler qualities the Afghans have no share. But they have strong passions, great thirst for love, and the freeman's respect for others' freedom. The woman is caressed and petted, loved with a passionate love, loaded with gifts, and then—when old age breaks her vigour—too often cast aside with the callous thoughtlessness of the savage. The men are jealous and she lives always under the shadow of a knife, the long, thin, sharp-edged knife of the Pathan, so quickly drawn across the throat at the first whisper of dishonour. Herself passionate and hot-tempered, she too blazes out in sudden rages, and the small dagger that she carries is not unseldom used. Passion and excitement, quick pulsing heart-beats, fiery love, splashing like scarlet flames upon the dusty background, and then the slow neglected downward track of old age, that is the Afghan woman's life.

Mostly she is chaste and clings to her own man, till the last bullet catches him full in the chest and his life gurgles out with the bubbling blood. But she can also love greatly and superbly, like the fine full-blooded creature that she is. There was such a girl once, a child merely, fifteen years old, who from the barred windows of her father's house at Kabul, saw a young English officer ride past on his charger with the ill-fated expedition. She came of royal stock and her father was a chieftain of rank in the Amir's service. Yet she learnt the officer's name, who can say with how many precautions and terrors: and found he was still unmarried. When the troops left, she crept forth too, this child of fifteen, and turned her face from her father's house and her people to follow the man she had chosen. She found her way across the mountains by the wind-bitten passes, with little food or shelter, till she reached the deserts of Sind and the wide stretches of the Indus. Not till then was she safe from the avenging dagger. Then slowly she traced her road till she came to the port of Karachi. And there, in the new cantonment, with its strange avenues and houses, she found the man whom she had sought. He, happily, was rich and of distinguished family. He heard her story and married the brave girl who had dared so much for his love. Then he brought her to England and had her taught and trained, and she found favour at Court, and their lives were happy.

Such the Afghan woman can be. The love which she gets—and gives—echoes in the poetry of Lawrence Hope.

> "You are all that is lovely and light,
> Aziza,—whom I adore,
> And, waking after the night,
> I am weary with dreams of you.
> Every nerve in my heart is tense and sore
> As I rise to another morning apart from you.
> I would burn for a thousand days,
> Aziza, whom I adore,
> Be tortured, slain, in unheard of ways
> If you pitied the pain I bore.
>
> . . . . . .
>
> Give me your love for a day,
> A night, an hour;
> If the wages of sin are death,
> I am willing to pay.
> What is my life but a breath
> Of passion burning away?
> Away from an unplucked flower?
> Oh! Aziza, whom I adore,
> Aziza, my one delight,
> Only one night—I will die before day,
> And trouble your life no more."

BORAH LADY FROM SURAT

The Hindu Woman in Marriage

ἀλλ' ἐννοεῖν χρὴ τοῦ το μὲν γυναῖχ' ὅτι
ἔφυμεν ὡς πρὸς ἄνδρας οὐ μαχουμίνα·
ἔ πει τα δ' οὕνεκ' ἀρχόμεσθ' ἐκ κρεισσόνων
καὶ ταῦ τ' ἀκούειν κἄτι τῶνδ' ἀλγίονα.

Antigone, ll. 61 *seq.*

"But we must reflect first that we were born a woman, Not such as to strive against men : and then that as we are ruled by them that are the stronger, we must obey in these things and in things yet sorer."

Chapter III

THE HINDU WOMAN IN MARRIAGE

MARRIAGE under the Hindu system is by no means easy to describe as in actual fact it is. The definitions and classifications given in the legal textbooks or Scriptures of the Hindus are little better than abstractions—deductions from assumed premisses of a theological kind, with only a slender tie to the actual life of Hindu societies. The difficulties of practice arise from the vast complexities and fluid conditions of the great masses of peoples and races, with divergent levels of culture and inconsistent ideas, that compose the aggregate which for convenience is distinguished from all others by the collective name of Hinduism. For Hinduism is, of course, in no real sense a church or creed. It has no definite tenets and no articles of dogma. The acceptance of a certain social system, centring upon the existence of hereditary priesthoods with divinely-given powers of interposition and interpretation, is its final criterion. This system and its practical consequences once accepted, the man is free to believe and follow what creeds or philosophies he may please.

Yet through it all there is a certain rather vague and elusive unity of idea, a spirit, one might say, that in various forms penetrates and transmutes the varying material of creed and caste, of blood and race with which it is presented. In essence this is the spirit which regards the whole world as an unreal dream, an illusory changing scene of transformations, stretched over the realities of a higher ultimate world of Divine unity. Laws and customs are based not on a reasoned pursuit of the good as existent in this life; but upon the means, magical or supernatural, of acquiring merit in a supposed ultimate universe of timeless and permanent reality reached after final severance from the circle of birth and death. It is a spirit diametrically opposed to that Greek thought which placed before man as his final and only aim happiness or the excellent performance of function in the world we know. Hardly less is it opposed to the Semitic creeds which project the purposes and rewards of virtue into a similar world of similar perceptions and individualities conceived as existent on a higher plane attainable after death. For the unifying spirit of Hinduism, so far as it can be grasped as in any way *one*, rejects the world altogether as a reality and places its virtues not in any reasoned balance of human rights and duties, but in the observance of rituals and austerities commended by the authority of a hierarchy.

Hence marriage also, as far as it approaches the ideal, is based upon considerations that are non-rational and belong rather to a mystical or supernatural way of regarding life. Marriage to the Hindu thinker and idealist has nothing to do, in its ultimate causes, with the preferences of one man or one woman, nothing to do with the pursuit of happiness in a palpitating finite and human life. He sees in it no free union of two human wills, joined for their own contentment in an isolated human relation. Rather it is the connection of two incarnations of the world spirit during an unreal moment of illusory existence. The proper husband and wife are recognized and selected by magical arts exercised under the authority of the Sacred Books by certain classes of the priesthood. They are joined under a right conjunction of the stars, interpreted by an hereditary expert in the magic art of astrology. Their marriage is sanctified by miraculous rites and blessed and transformed by the repetition of mysterious Sanskrit phrases. They enter their new state purified as by a consecration. In a word, they deal with a sacrament, not with a human contract. It is not the satisfaction of human feelings that is sought, but the fulfilment of a ritual duty to the family, in its relation to the Divine Spirit.

This view of marriage, as an ordained sacrament, is manifested throughout the actual ceremonies of the wedding, at least among the castes that claim the higher ritual ranks. The bride and bridegroom must belong to the same subdivision of the caste and yet must not be related by a common descent from the same mythical founder of the family. Before they can be betrothed, the horoscopes must be studied by an hereditary astrologer to see that the proposed union does not traverse any of the influences of the stars in their conjunctions. Nowadays it is true that horoscopes have fallen somewhat into neglect among the more "advanced." These allege that the time is wrongly found on any horologe except the old-fashioned water-clock and they insinuate—what is no doubt often true—that the verdict of the astrologer depends upon his emoluments. Thus even the most advanced of Hindus, if they do without such advice, do so on the ostensible ground that horoscopes are incorrectly delivered, not that in themselves they are unreasonable. Again the marriage is made between children, so that desire or personal preference shall not disturb the ordinances of heaven. The ceremony can take place only in the auspicious months when the constellations of Jupiter and Venus are in conjunction with the sun. At the wedding symbolic presentments of the boy's and girl's ancestors make more clear the significance of the wedding, as a mere phase in a family existence, in which the individual is as nothing and the race is all. When the moment approaches, the bride and bridegroom sit, face to face or side by side before the objects of worship, their right hands joined, a strand of red cotton round their necks, a cloth drawn as a screen between their faces. The priests chant Sanskrit verses, while the astrologer consults the water-clock, which is needed to read the exact sacerdotal hour. Then when the moment has come and the cloth is drawn, the pair turn round the sacred sacrificial fire, and the seven steps are taken which make the marriage indissoluble and eternal. The

A BRAHMAN LADY GOING TO THE TEMPLE

bridegroom turns to his wife and utters the sacred verse, "Oh! bride! give your heart to my work, make your mind agreeable to mine. May the God Brahaspati make you pleasing to me." Then for himself he swears not to transgress, whether for wealth or love. And then they go out and look upon the Polar Star, that star which guided the first Aryan wanderers across Asia.

A marriage of this kind, so solemn and so sacramental, cannot in the lifetime of its partakers be severed or dissolved. Only the will of God, executed by the cold scythe of Death, can grant a divorce. Until death come, the pair is inevitably joined, to labour and pray together, and to engender and bear the children who in time shall release their parents' souls from the purgatory of unfulfilled duties. The Hindu theory is a deduction from two principles, one, the unreality of individual appearance, the second, the unworthiness of sensuous illusion.

Marriage is a union of ephemeral beings for the sake of family and community, and for the attainment of a worshipful elevation over sense and the world of illusion. It is at once a consecration and an initiation. The absence of that strong sexual passion which we have clad in the jewelled veils of poetry and have baptized in the romantic waters of love is not to the Brahman eye an impediment or a disappointment. At the most the hope is for an ordered affection and a disciplined devotion.

But the facts of human nature cannot with impunity be ignored. Ideals based on a non-natural order of things may inspire noble poetry: but they must fail when they are applied to large bodies of men and women. Contracts founded upon causes and effects that are traced by reason can be applied without much hindrance and at any rate without hypocrisy by all those who can recognize facts. But there are few who are worthy of or can benefit by a sacrament. The Hindu spirit has created splendid images and has embodied in literature the characters of Sita and of Damyanti, the wife who is all devotion and sacrifice, nobly courageous, nobly patient. But, by its very distance from actuality, it leads in the practice of every day to great hypocrisy and unnecessary hardship. The danger has been foreseen by the lawgivers themselves: and they have not dared to apply their ideal, even in theory, to others than the highest castes of the hierarchy. For the warrior, the cultivator, and the menial classes they have allowed different practices and divergent ideals. Even in the practice of those Brahmans, to whom the system should apply in its entirety, considerable concessions have been authorized. In the unauthorized acts of every day life there are even greater deviations. In one sense, of course, it may be said that the theory of the highest Hinduism in regard to marriage is one and indivisible; but marriage is, after all, the concrete contact and companionship of a living, feeling man and woman, and the application of the theory an affair of national character. Race and climate and the influences of history have played their part in the Indian Continent at least as much as in other regions of equal area. Even in the priestly Brahman caste, the Brahman of the Deccan is as different from him of the Punjab as an Italian Marchese could be from a Prussian Graf. They come from different strains, they live in different surroundings: and the one bond is a common social system with some common ideals under which they have both obtained their power.

In general, it may be said that the ideal has been humanized and softened in all those parts of India in which Rajput or Mussulman influences have at any time been powerful. In such regions, in Gujarát, for instance, or in Káthiawád, the people have never taken kindly to the mere negation of desire. A certain practical genius has always turned their glance to the fruits of the earth and the pleasures of the senses. Commerce brought them wealth and the desire for comfort; from chivalry they learnt the lessons of gaiety and enjoyment. Among them beauty is esteemed and desired; pleasure sought or demanded. From a wife is expected charm and companionship, passion and pleasure. She is treated as a human being, with the ordinary human capacities and frailties; and she can exercise power and influence by her charms. She may be loved as a woman; and she is often the object of jealousy; but she is seldom deadened by that chilling respect which shrivels fresh desire.

In the arid, ascetic Deccan, on the other hand, the woman is more commonly disregarded. There she lives in an atmosphere where sensuousness is reproached, though it may be practised. A man indulges passion, if he do so at all, as a thing shameful in itself and abominable, with stealth and self-abasement, in the grossest and least urbane manner. If he yield to a sexual desire, it is without esteem or regard for the partner in his sin. Towards the wife of a consecrated marriage he preserves an attitude, which may be irreproachable, but must certainly be unflattering to her womanhood. In the light of religion, she may be regarded as a partner in a mystic union : but in the household she is often little better than a housekeeper, contemned, neglected, and never warmed by the glow of desire nor wooed with those attentions by which men seek to please. Between Gujarát and the Deccan, it is again the contrast, only intensified, between France and England. On the one hand, power and pleasure and the charm of life—with perhaps jealousy and a certain sense of the possibilities of human frailty. On the other, coldness, a real contempt, and that callous reliance on an unswerving chastity, which some have been pleased to call respect—and which is so annoying even to the plainest woman.

Religion again effects a distinction. Those who adhere to the worship of Shiva, the God of Destruction, the Lord of Death, the Master of Ascetics, are apt to turn from the goods of this life to a final absorption in an abstract oneness. But in Krishna, the very human incarnation of God the Preserver, the inhabitants of the richer and more fertile tracts of the continent have found a congenial saviour.

From the devotees of his creed he demands only love, a constant and all-absorbing offering of the heart: and he bestows upon them in return the free ease of the world through which they are passing on the way to the love-laden groves of Paradise. While the followers of the theology that centres upon Shankar see the universe as one, an abstract God-in-himself, indivisible, unchanging, a pure spirit that alone *is* and has being, and define the aim of life as, after reiterated births into further action, the final liberation from the senses by absorption into this infinite and unqualified spirit, the worshippers of Krishna adopt a teaching which admits an eternal dualism. Force and nature, spirit and matter, are to them an everlasting pair, which can never be finally united. So they tend readily to a view of life in which man and the Deity, as he can know Him, are circumscribed by nature, and in which man can find salvation in the love of all things. And in the love of all things, if there be inward grace, the enjoyment of the nature that God has granted to the world must be allowable. Freedom is attained when the enjoyment is unconditioned and the soul is wholly united to the spirit of all nature. It is only the conditions of life, and the need for transcending the wants of the world in order to reach that grace in which God is directly felt, which can impose restrictions and prohibitions. So, naturally enough, the disciple of the gracious, kind, and loving Krishna is more likely to demand love from the companion of life than the ascetic votary of Shiva.

The practical meaning of marriage is again very different in the warrior caste, now represented by the Rajput clans. Comparatively recent invaders of mixed Scythian and Turkish or Hunnish tribes, they almost alone in India have become what in Europe is meant by a gentry or an aristocracy. Feudal in their concept of the state, cavaliers and men-at-arms, seeking in war a profession, in the acquisition of landed estates their fulfilment, and in sport their relaxation, they have brought to the brown monotony of India the splendour of gallantry, chivalry, and romance. Exempted even by priestly ordinance from the oppressive asceticism that is in general obligatory to the Hindu mind, they have formed for themselves a code of honour coloured by the legitimate hopes and enjoyments of a warrior clan. In the traditions of their caste they still preserve the memory of the bride's choosing. The suitors sat assembled, each in his own place, in the palace hall, with sword and shield to his hand. The curtain was uplifted and the bride stepped round the hall, a garland of flowers on her arm. Then when she reached the man whom she chose to be her own prince and beloved husband, she slipped the garland on his neck. Thus they became man and wife, and no one could deny their will. That time is long since gone, and no bride has now such a choosing. Yet to this day the heroines of all Indian plays and the great women of Indian poetry are all of the Rajput class. Marriage is with them even now a practice adapted to the aristocratic temper partly from the earlier Brahman books and partly from the traditions of Central Asia, tinged also by the fashions set by Mussulman emperors in the Courts at Delhi. Polygamy is recognized as lawful and is practised by the Ruling Chiefs and the richer of their cadets. The maid-servant may be the concubine of her master and the dancing girl who enlivens the Courts is often in private a mistress. But great is the power of the wife behind the curtain, deep and warm-blooded the love she hopes to win, great also her valorous devotion. And through the whole fabric runs a woof as of old, half-faded brocade, a thread of chivalry and pure reverence and protective delight. A strand of silk at the wrist may make the Rajput gentleman at any moment the knight-errant of a lady whom he shall never see, and for whom his honour shall yet be as a brother's.

But to the Rajput lady of a ruling house there is one special terror. If death puts his finger on her husband, her life is too often overwhelmed to an extent unnecessary and cruel. For herself remarriage is forbidden: and a love-affair is often requited with secret poison by her husband's successors. For there are many who still hold that the family honour can be stained indelibly by a woman's lightness. Then in her husband's place may sit on the throne a rival's son, who from childhood has had his ears filled with bitterness. Her jointure may be insufficient; even an administration is only too often unsympathetic or unduly sparing of money; or the successor may by force or intrigue attenuate the estate that was bequeathed. She finds interest no doubt in the management of the lands that form her jointure, but her seclusion places her largely in the hands of interested advisers. As a rule, the downfall is more lamentable even than that of the Dowager in Europe, except perhaps in Royal families. Suicide (*Sati*) on the funeral pyre was in the past almost a release for the Rajput widow. Among the smaller Rajput yeomanry, the case is better. Remarriage is not unseldom allowed. At the worst, the wife has had no rival and her own child succeeds ; while, failing children, she finds with her relatives the respect and kindness to women which is general in this caste of manly gentlemen.

Another group consists of the lower, but thoroughly Hinduized, working castes. These run from the very low untouchable castes who are the usual domestics of the European officer to the skilled artisan and the cultivator. Their matrimonial regulations are a compromise (like most compromises hardly " working ") between Brahman theory, economic necessity, and obsolete primitive custom. They are influenced vaguely by the usual ideals. Widow remarriage is however tolerated and commonly practised, though somewhat looked down upon in the popular regard. When the parties to the association are working men and women, miserably poor for the most part, illiterate and unprogressive, it follows naturally that the action of the system is conditioned mainly by economics. Toil and labour, in field or factory or shop, is the part of both, and the woman's household work and the

FROM JODHPUR

assistance of the growing children are incentives to and conditions of the marriage. They have no leisure for the finer sensibilities and, like the poor in all countries, must have an eye ever open to the needs of food and nutrition. Without much education and with little capacity for refined emotion, it is not unnatural if there is sometimes disunion, and if they seldom attain the heights. The husband in his cups may occasionally beat his wife, or may have to sit with bowed head before the storm of her boisterous abuse. Yet they compare favourably with similar classes in other countries; and at the worst they shame the terrors of European slums, the brutal wife-kickers and procurers who lurk in the blind alleys of industrial life. It is true indeed that the rapid growth of industrial labour in India also has adversely affected the marriages of that class and that only too often an unhappy union ends in elopement or prostitution. Generally, however, it may be said that the Hindu husband even in this class seldom descends to the grossness and cruelty so often found in the lower quarters of European cities: while the wife forms and maintains a higher standard of womanly conduct and devotion. An easier toleration marks their conjugal relations and the Hindu character at its worst is commonly free from the extremer modes of brutality.

Among the aboriginal tribes, the Bhils for instance, marriage is still in a very fluid condition. The actual form that in practice it takes depends inevitably on the extent to which the tribe has succumbed to

Hindu or rather Brahman influence. As it becomes subjected to that influence, and as in consequence it aims at raising its rank within the Hindu social system by the aping of higher castes, so it the more readily adopts the worst accretions to Hindu matrimony, child-marriage, for instance, and large dowries. But in general it may be said that marriage among such tribes is a free association between youthful adults, promulgated by certain payments of money or service to the bride's parents and relieved, if barren or unhappy, by an almost unrestricted right of divorce. Pre-nuptial chastity is hardly looked for, and neither man nor girl is much blamed for an early slip. After marriage chastity is the usual rule. The attitude is in practice not very dissimilar from the reasonable and natural outlook of the Scottish peasant; and, as in Scotland, the net result is a state of general happiness, easy and equal companionship, and very remarkable mutual trust. The woman has much weight in affairs and not unfrequently holds the purse. As in the country districts of Scotland, prostitution is unknown, and the cruel ruin of a woman who has loved too soon is practically unheard of. Widows of course remarry, and there is much homely love between husband and wife and parents and children.

Another system still survives among the inhabitants of the southern coast lands where the Arabian Sea beats against the palm groves of Malabar. Here the tribes of the Nairs, formerly warlike and still brave, headed by the ruling house of Travancore, maintain a marriage system that dates from the earlier Dravidian culture which preceded the Aryan invasions. Both among the Nairs—the noble class—and among the priests, the Nambutiri Brahmans, an ecclesiastical and land-owning aristocracy of peculiar sanctity, the customs of matriarchy prevail in various degrees. Among the Nairs, for several centuries, the law was of polyandry, pure and simple, the wife having several husbands according to her own good pleasure. In late years the actual habit of polyandry is to all intents defunct and only in very few cases, if at all, could a Nair lady be found who consorts with more than one husband. But succession is still traced through the female line and a boy succeeds to his mother's brother, not to his father. And in other subtler ways the effects of polyandry are still manifest. Perhaps the most curious survival is that the religious ceremonial of marriage—an expensive and public rite—is performed at an early age with a man, with whom the girl has no other connection than formal participation in this ineffective sacrament. Much later comes what, in the European sense, would be called the real marriage, with the husband whom she is to cherish. This is a contract, entered into freely by both parties, dissoluble at will. One of the elements of its popularity and success is in this very freedom which has given the Nair ladies a position enjoyed by few other Indian women. An attempt absurdly made to limit this freedom by legislation, which gave an option to the parties by an act of registration to introduce the usual disabilities of a rigid matrimony, has proved an utter failure. An accompaniment of the polyandrous or matriarchal system, which still prevails, is that husband and wife do not live together. The Nair house is the abode of a whole large family, based upon joint descent from a common female ancestor. In the house or family mansion the apartments of the women are together and are entirely separate from that part of the house in which the men live. In this house the husband has no part or share; but he comes to visit his wife in her apartment just as she goes occasionally to visit him in the similar household in which, by his descent on the mother's side, he has a right to live. On the freedom of choice exercised by a Nair lady in her mating there is little restriction, save only the one that she must not choose a man of lower station.

The Nambutiri Brahmans, on the other hand, though they live among the Nair tribes and are their priests, have gone no further than a compromise between this system and the arrangements usually prevalent among Brahmans. The results, like those of most compromises, have been disastrous. Only the eldest son of a family marries. The rest, when study of Scripture and the practice of ascetic simplicity prove unsatisfying, seek consolation in indiscriminate seduction. The immediate results of a theory so unnatural are polygamy, burdensome dowries, marriages for wealth alone, and the seclusion and bondage of women. In spite of the simplicity and candour of these Brahmans—qualities which make them personally loveable even to those who deplore their influence—their community has been gravely injured by such marriages. Only the simplicity of their desires and the earnest conservatism of their faith have made them tolerate a system so unnatural and injurious. They bow with pious resignation to the will of God, by which they mean the results of their own human folly.

Bitter must the contrast be to the secluded and austere Nambutiri ladies when they see their Nair neighbours at the annual winter festival which commemorates the death of Kámdev, the Hindu God of Love. Long before daybreak, every Nair girl of any position is out of bed and goes with her girl friends to the nearest tank. Plunging into the water together, they sing in unison the song which is sacred to the God of human hearts. As they sing, they beat the water, with the left hand held immediately under the surface and the right brought down upon it in a sloping stroke, splashing and sounding deep. Stanza after stanza, song after song they sing till the first light of dawn peeps over the cocoanut palms. Then they go back to their homes to dress in their best and enjoy their holy day. They darken their eyelids with collyrium and make their lips red with betel leaf. In the gardens they play on swings with their friends. Then they sit down in merriment and enjoyment to the noon-day meal of arrowroot and molasses with ripe yellow plantains and green cocoanuts. Afterwards they again sing and dance, while all good husbands on this day of days visit their wives in their family mansions and make themselves pleasant to the ladies of the family and bring little presents and friendly good wishes.

This system, strange though it appears to those who are familiar only with Jewish and Teutonic customs, has been particularly successful in securing the ends of every marriage—comfort, free development, and the worthy upbringing of healthy children. In no class in India is education better appreciated and more widely shared by the sexes. Every Nair girl is sent to the village school, her education as much a matter of course as her brothers'; while there are many who have matriculated at the Madras University. At the same time, by the universal admission of those who know them, there are few women in India who have greater charm or exercise as valuable an influence on the manners and morals of society.

Marriage in Hindu India is, therefore, very various both in practice and in theory according to the locality and the race or caste. But regarded as a whole it presents, one may say, some common characteristics. It is invariably a religious rite, sanctioned by magical ceremony, really sacramental. Only in castes which allow a widow to remarry is the second union divested of most of this supernatural sanction, to become almost a free contract. Again marriages are in general arranged by the parents or relations—with the advice of priests and astrologers—while the husband and wife are still children, either in real childhood or shortly after their puberty. Further, in all the higher castes, and in lower castes as they assume or usurp a higher position, widows are forbidden a further marriage. Normally the idea of marriage in the classes in which Brahman influence is most firm is accompanied by a certain ascetic thought, which holds sensuousness and enjoyment to be something debasing and earth-bound. The world of action being illusory and unreal, and each action entailing its answering reaction, deliverance from illusive appearances and absorption into the one final reality can be gained only by passive withdrawal from activity. But all action springs from desire: and the strongest and most attractive of desires is love. Hence in marriage there should be no overpowering desires, none of those impulses of emotion which keep the man bound during thousands of incarnations to the idly-turning wheel of illusion. Only as a deliverance from conflicting desire and as the means of continuing family life is marriage in itself to be valued. Its happiness and fruition are to be sought not in the tumults of passion but in the calm and ordered affection of a disciplined and worshipful pair. From the husband protection and self-restraint are due; from the wife to the lord, whom heaven has given her, unflinching devotion, constant respect and obedience, unwavering chastity.

But in some castes and places the ideal has been altered largely by feudalism and chivalry, by luxury and an appreciation of human happiness, and by the influences of a kindly humanizing belief. There we find love welcomed and pursued, and the beauteous wife elevated like a substantiation of that Krishna-spirit in which man attains on earth to the love which is unending.

In general, Hindu marriage does undoubtedly, to a marked extent, reach very closely to the purposes which it seeks. In general, it produces a very real, if somewhat colourless, affection, an affection maintained by common interests and the great bond of constant association. The defects which it has are in the main the excrescences of a religious system, such as are apt to grow wherever reason is displaced by theological or supernatural commandment. When rationalism grows strong enough to question the authority of priestly ordinance and tradition, it will be possible without any very serious effort to prune them safely from the sturdy trunk of Hindu life.

Child-marriage is, of course, that one of all its features which has been most violently attacked. But it may be doubted whether those who have attacked it have always had a clear understanding of its significance. Real child-marriage—the wedding of children who have not yet reached puberty—is after all nothing more than an indefeasible betrothal. And in itself it is a logical and natural deduction from a theory which postulates the selection of the bridal pair by supernatural agency, working either through the divinations of an astrologer or through the parents' careful affection. Any element of personal choice and free-will would be repugnant to the underlying thoughts and must to a large extent be subversive of

A MILL-HAND

the social and moral superstructure. Free-choice could be introduced generally only by a substitution for Brahman regulation of something quite other—as the warrior castes, for instance, extorted for themselves from a submissive hierarchy a different scale of moral values. Moreover, in practice child-marriage has some clear advantages. For it allows the wedded pair to be brought up together, as children only, in their parents' houses, till in time they become habituated to each other's company and affection, while gradually they come to know and learn their place in those large households to which their future lives belong. The Hindu married couple can live in no independent isolation like the European. Rather they will be but one unit of a great family household managed on behalf of all by its eldest members. The real marriage, the consummation of their growth to man and woman, comes much later, after many years perhaps, when the parents at last give their consent to the grown student and the healthy maiden who helps daily in the household tasks. Rather it is not the child-marriage that is so much to be deprecated as the marriage that succeeds, as in some castes it does, too quickly upon puberty. For, by an unhappy ignorance, puberty is in India only too often thought, as it was thought in the Europe of the Renaissance, to be maturity; and the marriage thus concluded is at once made real.

In fact, in both cases what is needed is a little more scientific knowledge and the embodiment of the knowledge in the Penal Code. Cases occur only too frequently of the martyrdom of young brides, not so much from cruelty, or even from uncontrolled passion, as from sheer ignorance of scientific fact. It has become a superstition, supported of course by the usual authority, that puberty means maturity, not merely for love—which would be sufficiently misleading—but even for child-bearing. Here it is that rational education must enter the field. In a country in which knowledge is luckily not accounted shameful, it is easy for education to explain that puberty is only the beginning of a new period, and that love's first blossoms must not be followed by too early fruit.

In this respect the practice of Hindu marriage unhappily does show a fault of the most serious and terrible kind. If education has still much to do, the state of the law most certainly requires improvement. It is sometimes said that the Penal Law of India at present does not give adequate protection to girls who, for various reasons, are unmarried. But silence is usually kept about the far more serious fact that it provides practically no protection to the married girl. In her case the age of consent has actually been fixed at twelve; and no child of more than twelve can claim protection from the law against the brutality of the man to whom she has been married. Obviously the limit of age for the protection of girls should be the same in all cases, whether she be married or unmarried, whether she be the victim of the man to whom she has been joined beside the sacred fire or of one who owes her no special duty. It is the most obvious confusion of thought which fails to see that the offence, if it is one, is exactly the same, whether or not a mystical ritual has been first observed. The *thug* was no better than a common strangler because he first prayed to Bhavani before he murdered. The offence is the same in all cases ; the punishment should, if anything, be more severe to the man who is peculiarly bound in duty and in honour to cherish the woman he has made his wife. The State is now prepared to protect against perversion a class of women who, on an outside estimate, do not exceed one-hundredth of the population and who *ex hypothesi* are of a position and character somewhat less than reputable. But the State denies its protection to the other ninety-nine women of each hundred, the mothers of the country, the honoured helpmates of its households.

The harshness is made the greater by vices which, though forbidden, have in practice become common. The sale of daughters is an offence against which the sacred writings of the Hindus strongly and consistently inveigh. Yet in only too many cases parents do little else than sell their girls in marriage to the highest bidder. The sums of money which they demand and which they use, not for the daughter's benefit, but for their own, are so large that they are forced to accept a suitor of sufficient substance without regard to fitness or religious sanction. Of the higher classes many nowadays revolt against such conduct, which they recognize to be wicked and despicable. But in the lower castes it is still general. The inner motive of such actions is, of course, the ignorance, quite as much as the selfishness, of the father. Too ignorant to comprehend that a human soul is an end in itself and that a daughter is also a free human being, he looks on her with besotted eye as a mere instrument of his own betterment. Hand in hand with this evil, and dependent from it, is the terrible practice of giving young brides to elderly husbands. In no other country could the results be more disastrous or the girl-wife more unhappy. Vallabh, the Gujaráti poet, has expressed that wretchedness in a beautiful song, which has had some influence in abating this social evil. From it the following lines are quoted, addressed to the Goddess Mother :—

> " Goddess mother, old is the husband thou hast given me,
> Mother, accursed is this coming to life of mine. Alas, what more can I say ?
> Goddess mother, a little child am I and he a great lumbering, aged man,
> My youth is like a blossom and my husband is a shrivelled mummy.
> Mother, mine are just sixteen years and he has seen his eighty.
> Goddess mother, of a winter's night there is many a taste one feels,
> But doltish is old age, and my husband is deaf and dumb.
> Goddess mother, sportive am I and would like to play and I make my eyes twinkle,
> But, mother, he, he says, 'I'll beat you,' and lifts his stick in his hand.
> Old is my husband, mother, what good can come out of age ?

Goddess mother, on the festival all the girls are gaily dressed and merry,
But my husband is tired and weak and ugly, and I bend my head in shame.
Mother, my hair is black and his head is all white or grey.
My youth is at its blooming and already my life is wrecked.
Goddess mother, why was I not strangled at birth, why was I not poisoned?
Yet if my husband die, it is my part to be true to death.
Nay, Goddess mother, with joined hands I pray at thy feet,
When I am born again, give me a husband that is young and strong."

But as long as society tolerates the acceptance of money by a bride's father, so long will there be parents to be tempted by gold to sanction their children's ruin. And even then there will persist a deeper reason. For girls are all early married and widows may not marry a second time. So, even against his will, an elderly man is forced, if he wishes to have the legitimate and socially-sanctioned companionship of a woman, to seek in marriage one of the young girls who alone are in India available for a suitor.

The prohibition of widow remarriage has also been bitterly attacked, often by those Indians who, from education or environment, have been affected by rationalism, sometimes by those who find a false pride in the imitation of foreign custom. But the prohibition is not of course universal. Those castes which have not yet set up a claim to the higher ceremonial purities, are free to compound with human desires by a second marriage, devoid of sacramental significance. It is in the higher classes that the woman may have to pay for the pride of caste by her individual austerities. Yet against the prohibition of widow remarriage may be set the terrific wastage in Europe of chaste and unmarried women. It has not at least entailed upon Indian society that narrowing and unnatural education which Europe has seen itself forced to accept, with all its consequent evils, and which is perhaps inevitable if chastity is to be required as their highest and sometimes their only virtue from women who are in every case condemned to a lengthy and, in a vast number of unhappy cases, to a life-long celibacy. In India a woman is at least allowed to *know* and to be natural; for an early marriage gives her in her ripening maturity the fitting fulfilment of her womanhood. And, even at the worst conjunction of destiny, the ideal of devotion crystallized in an unbroken widowhood is, in itself, no ignoble aspiration. The unflinching veneration that a son gives to his widowed mother is in India no small recompense for her sacrifice to a sacred duty. Widowhood is recognized by all as a state—divinely imposed—of austerity and atonement. But it has its own quiet rewards in the family home, with its sense of duty done, like a nun's or a Sister of Mercy's. It is harsh in those castes, which have merely adopted a custom, when the inspiring ideal is not felt living in their hearts, deep and intense. And it is also harsh in those cases where the original thought has been warped by an exaggerated deduction or where punishment is too rigorously exacted for illicit infringement of the rule. At least in the case of the child-widow, betrothed indeed by a sacrament, but never really wedded, some speedy relaxation of the rule appears desirable: and it is probable that, with the decay of faith and with the new scepticism about blessings conveyed by an astrologer's predictions, some such amendment will soon ensue.

A deeper objection to the Hindu system is one which has been seldom, if ever, expressed. Racially, the absence of that natural selection which expresses itself in sexual desire, cannot but be detrimental. It is perhaps vain to expect a vigorous childhood to be born from unions in which healthy desire is replaced by the coldness of duty or by an instinct that has not been transfigured by personal attraction and selection. The difficulty is inherent in a system which bases its selection upon the supernatural and rejects the natural call of spirit to spirit and sense to sense. And yet it must be confessed, not without shame, that a careful selection by parents, if it could be trusted to be rational and disinterested, might be no more injurious than the restricted and illusory choice, too often made in ignorance, which so far seems to be the only substitute that civilization has learnt to provide. In general, it may be said that the Hindu rules of marriage are, in the ordinary sense of happiness, as conducive to the happiness of the spouses as the fast transforming systems of modern Europe, and that their happiness is less self-centred and more altruistic. Romantic love is, after all, most commonly, even in Europe, the short-lived flower of life in one sex and one class. Marriage must everywhere be in practice limited and artificially restricted. Economic conditions are very near the base of most marriages; and even in the richer classes must be a main constituent of the bride's decision. Moreover, for the lasting purposes of marriage, affection is no bad substitute for love—affection and the sense of destined consecration. It may at least be asserted that, in general, among the upper castes of India the mingled feeling of duty and devotion is as strong as, and perhaps more stable than, in the corresponding sections of English society. In many places, however, and in many castes, the soft bloom of companionship and emotion is bruised by the brutality of a first union with a partner before unknown and undesired. Nor can it be denied that the gnostic asceticism, to which Indian idealism has so often condescended, has killed, where it could, that joy in a free humanity which alone can invest marriage with the flaming beauty of love. When the value of love is considered as an inspiration to art and chivalry and, indeed, to every creative activity, then the loss, thus self-inflicted, will appear in all its gravity. It may well be that the deathly slumber of the arts in modern India is to no small extent due to spiritual conditions which exclude and condemn the love which is profane, and is therefore alive and immortal.

A MAHAR WOMAN

The Ladies of the Aristocracy

“ Love in full life and length, not love ideal,
No, nor ideal beauty, that fine name,
But something better still, so very real
That the sweet model must have been the same.

. . . . .

And oh ! the loveliness at times we see
In momentary gliding, the soft grace,
The youth, the bloom, the beauty which agree,
In many a nameless being we retrace,
Whose course and home we know not nor shall know
Like the lost Pleiad seen no more below.”

Beppo. Lord Byron.

Chapter IV

THE LADIES OF THE ARISTOCRACY

WHAT exactly it is which constitutes an aristocracy, at any given time or place, is not always easy to define. In Europe, in general, aristocracies are based upon the survivals of feudal fiefs or sometimes upon Court distinctions—but how greatly altered, broadened, twisted, and transmuted! In India special considerations have arisen to complicate the question. For all through Indian society there run, on different curves, double classifications, each traced by divergent forces. On the one hand, as in all human societies—unhappily imperfect—lies the great universal distinction which one calls rank, distinction of power, that is, and official authority, with distinction of wealth as accompaniment or even as sole qualification. On the other side lie the less natural —shall they be called unnatural ?—distinctions of a hierarchic classification, peculiar to this continent and the Hindu faith. In this hierarchy, the classification is not by power as tested and exercised in the world, open and plain to all men, but by a claim to power over supernatural forces, acquired by religious merit, not necessarily in the individual life but perhaps in lives assumed to have occurred in past transmigrations. But, as the saint spends in study and prayer the hours during which conquerors are active with sword or sceptre, so religious merit does not necessarily bring wealth or authority—with which indeed it should be incompatible. Moreover, religious austerities and abnegations spring from or produce a character, to which the vices and virtues of a feudal aristocracy are alike opposed. So though the Brahman is in the hierarchy of caste by universal recognition infinitely the highest, so much indeed above all others as to be by mystic ordinance "twice-born," though he is ceremonially pure as purity itself, though his life is sacred and his blessing a reward, his curse a menace and a doom, yet in no actual sense can his caste be said to form an aristocracy. A few there are among the caste who have risen to royal state and rule lands as princes; but even in them the qualities of human leadership are overwhelmed by the traditions of a scholar race and a consecrated people.

Actually, therefore, it may be said—if words are used in the usual sense—that the aristocracy of India is composed of the Mussulman nobility and of the second or Kshatriya class of Hindus, the ruling and fighting houses of the land. And of these at once the most interesting and the most important are the tribes known collectively under the name of Rajputs, "sons of kings," as the word would read in English. They are, of all the people of India, the most gallant and picturesque. Almost they are Indian chivalry itself.

The Ladies of the Aristocracy

In India, the homes properly speaking of the Rajput tribes are in Márwár, Mewár, and Káthiawád, in the tracts, that is, which stretch from the centre of the Continent to the sands of Sind and down to the base of the Peninsula, as well as in the province that projects into the Ocean to the West. From the desert of Bikanir and Jodhpur, where water has to be sought by shafts hundreds of feet below the level of the scorching sand, to the forests and glens and rocks of Mewár and to the fertile plains that roll across Gujarát to the Arabian Sea, they rule or hold their lands on service tenures, and hunt and shoot and make love and yearn for battle. Bikanir, Jodhpur, Rutlam, Jamnagar, Baria, and how many other names there are that in the Great War have made dear the Rajput clans! They have borne the flag as fighting gentlemen to France and Flanders, to East Africa, and the plains of the Tigris and Euphrates. The recital of their deeds and glory is a task, alas! for other pens. Be it for these lines to make something plain of the manner of their daily life at home.

But first a few words must be written of their history. For without some such knowledge, there can be no understanding either of India or of the qualities for which the Rajput stands. Modern India, as it is now known, came to shape in the nine hundred or thousand years that passed from the day of Alexander to the Mussulman conquests. Before that period there was an India, still reflected in the Scriptures and in the living beliefs of the people, when Aryan immigrants furnished rulers and priests to dark Dravidian masses, cousins of those who still people the South Sea Archipelagoes, peoples who even now form the staple of the Southern Indian population, those who speak Tamil and Telugu and migrate as labourers not only to Ceylon but even to Fiji and Jamaica and Trinidad. But after the division of Alexander's Eastern Empire, that vast half-obscure series of invasions began which changed the face of the greater part of the Indian continent and altered all the constituents of its population. From the Bactrian Empire and its Hellenized inhabitants, came Menander with the Ionians—Yávans as they are known in Indian history. From the Oxus valley and Central Asia came the Scythian Sákas and the Kusháns. And all of these accepted the Buddhist faith and ruled kingdoms and helped learning and founded new families. Then, in the end of the fourth and throughout the fifth centuries, this India already so transformed, was flooded by the vaster, all transmuting hordes of Gujjars and White Huns. Each horde in turn swept into its embrace something of its predecessors, each being widely mixed and composite. So to the last in all those conquering peoples—and the Huns were a people on the move and not an army —there were elements of Greek and Turk, Ávar and Mongol, and Persian and Caucasian—all the elements in short that go also to make up Eastern Europe and its nations. Those were the peoples from whom descend the Kshatriya caste of modern India, these fine well-mannered fiery sportsmanlike Rajputs, who are the pride of their country. They look like any Hungarian nobleman or Georgian chief; and all the centuries spent in enervating climates and an austere faith have not taken from them their dash and passionate fervour.

They are Kshatriyas now, it has been said, these Rajputs from Central Asia. For from of old the classic, if academic, division of the Indian peoples has been supposed to be in four great caste or class abstractions, of which the second or warrior class is known as Kshatriya. And in fact it was into this caste that the invaders were by artful priests assumed to be adopted. The first hordes, from Bactria and the Oxus, had become followers of Buddha, a casteless faith in which the Brahman priesthood lost its privileges. But the later comers, the Gujjars and Huns, with their adoration of fire and sun and moon, were quickly persuaded to the Hindu system and the acceptance of the Brahman priesthood. So they slew as they conquered and extirpated the adherents of the reformed creed. And for reward they obtained the rank of Kshatriya and genealogies of the true Aryan breed. Those who were soldiers and founded states or formed the fighting men-at-arms of the clan maintained the rank, and are the Rajputs of to-day. The rest, as they settled down to trade or craftsmanship or as each by the succeeding horde was engulfed, and, where it was not absorbed, oppressed, brought to the multitudinous castes of upper India that

Rajput element which is still strongly marked by Scythian tribal names and even by customs or appearance. It was a clan system, something like the Highland clans. Just as Macdonalds or Camerons absorbed into themselves earlier Picts or later broken septs, so did even the proud Sesodias of Udepur, one must suppose, take into their tribe in the first rush of conquest many converted Sákas or Kusháns, broken tribes, it may be, who were useful recruits, or perhaps at times some powerful leaders. As the Highlander going to Glasgow or the Lowlands, lost his nobility and became artisan or weaver or tradesman, marrying with the common people and shedding his pride and distinctions, so of the Central Asian fighting tribes there were many who descended to the common level of the working population.

Now the Rajput tribes for over a thousand years have been the kernel of Indian aristocracy. They have lofty genealogies which trace their trees to roots in mythology, to birth from fire or the personified sun and moon. The god Krishna, a Kshatriya chief, indeed, of real but hidden fact, mixed inextricably with the ancient concept of a cloud-god, powerful in some forgotten Aryan home, has his place as divine progenitor in many a family tradition. They have their professional bards who sing the epics of their race and preserve the records of their families and descent. For a thousand years they have spent the lustres fighting, tumultuous, each chief with his following against his neighbour, always divided, yet throughout

LADY FROM MEWAR

in no mere lust of acquisition but in the spirit of a sport, sought for its own sake, governed by the rules of chivalry. Throughout Rajputana and Káthiawád, their castles stand on every eminence. Thence they could sally forth upon a foray, or in them, if the worst befell, sustain a brief siege. Younger sons either went out to carve themselves a career and perhaps a kingdom with the sword or received an appanage, half-independent, in which they governed as vassal princes. The chief ruled with a power absolute and arbitrary; but he had to rule as a father among his children. The clan obeyed, as a child obeys his father; yet withal there was always a curious feeling of equality. They were all of the same blood, they felt, high or low, born to carry arms, all gentlemen; and the chief was no better than his poorest brother, except that God had given him as eldest of the older line the right of decision in affairs. For their estates the clansmen paid by service, each according to his fief serving in person or with subordinate horsemen and men-at-arms. To this class belong the women who have been India's heroines, the women whose names survive in story, brave with the brave, tender and true. Best known of all, perhaps too well-known again to bear mention, are Padmini, the princess of Mewár, and her no less courageous companions and maid-servants. For she was beautiful, of a beauty so surpassing as to bring ruin to her own people. 'Alá-ud-din, the great conqueror, heard of her fame and contrived to see her features in a mirror. Then, having looked, he swore that she must be yielded to his passion or, if not, that Chitor, the capital of Mewár, should fall. Finally, when it was no longer possible to resist and the impregnable fort was only too clearly pregnable by the enemy, Padmini called the wives and daughters of the fighting men and told them what was in her mind. In the vaults deep within the core of this strange hill fortress, they piled wood and straw and built themselves a vast pyre. Then with a farewell to the soldiers who were to charge in one last sortie upon the enemy, the women went down the steps to the supreme offering and laid themselves upon the logs of burning wood and died. In this way the women of Chitor—without one to shrink or to draw back—preserved for all time the memory of Rajput honour and the exaltation of Rajput womanhood.

Even to-day, without a doubt, there are within the *zanánas* of Mewár many women of a spirit no less sublime. The honour of the family, that is a sacred flame which they feed in their hearts with ever renewed fuel of self-sacrifice and devotion. That is a repute, which, even when they sin, they seek to preserve intact; and they know only too well that infraction of this law brings with it death. The women live, with few exceptions, in the strictest seclusion, seeing no male person except their husband and occasionally an uncle or a brother. But, in despite of privacy, the fame of their conduct is whispered abroad and their influence in affairs is only too often felt, even by Political Agents and Residents. In a chief's household, there may be two or three wives, each with her separate establishment and her appanages. The management of her estates alone demands a good deal of intelligence and force of will. Handicapped as she is by being forced to converse with her stewards through a curtain, behind which she remains invisible, it is remarkable with what ability many a Rajput wife or widow controls the administration of her funds, though sometimes unhappily she may become the victim of fraud or specious appearances. The popular estimation of the Rajput ladies' talents is shown in the Gujaráti proverb, "The clever woman's children are fools, and the foolish woman's children are clever," in which the former is the Rajput woman with her impetuous and often imprudent sons, and the latter the cunning Bania trader with his usually awkward and futile mother.

Only experience can show how deep, and sometimes how perverted, is the respect for family honour; how hard the duty imposed upon women to preserve it above all things else at any cost. Some years ago, a young Rajput gentleman in an access of insane rage murdered his stepmother in her room. He had a sister, a girl of eighteen, still unmarried, who was sitting beside the pair and saw the murder done before her eyes. As it happened, a Government officer was near the place, got early information, and by a forced ride through darkness over forest tracks was able to reach the scene of the murder by midnight. He went at once to the girl's quarters and, while respecting the custom of purdah, insisted upon speaking to her in person. The girl was still shaken by the murder that she had witnessed, her nerves upset, her night sleepless, her mind a vortex of cruel impressions. Under the skilful questioning, she soon broke down, and—told the truth! She recounted the facts as they had happened; and the facts were that her brother, the head of the family, was a murderer. But thereafter the girl remained unmarried, no Rajput of lineage, however poor, being found to accept in marriage a Rajput maiden who by the mere truth had fixed in the public eye a stain on the family name.

Of Rajput wooings there is still many a romantic story to be told. In one of the smaller states there had been some talk of marrying the daughter of the house to a greater chief. The young lady, a girl of about fifteen, exceptionally beautiful and graceful, well-educated, a writer of excellent letters both in her own and in the English language, managed to get hold of a photograph of the proposed consort and incontinently fell in love with the pictured image. The negotiations met with unexpected difficulties and the project all but fell through. The young chief, who had not seen her, was indifferent and accepted an offer from a more powerful state, where he married the young princess, almost a child. This was so far from damping the other lady, that it served only to inflame her further. The greater the difficulty, the more determined she was to win the man whom she now loved with a bitter passion. She wrote, she intrigued, she guided the negotiations herself, she entreated and schemed and insisted. At last she was successful, and the young chief came to wed her as his second wife. Throughout the ceremony, he was indifferent, almost bored. From his manner it was plain that he married only as a duty, because he was a gentleman, bound to a promise which he may have thought himself cheated into giving. But, the ceremony over, he went according to custom to eat the first meal with his new wife and for the first time to see her face and listen to her speech. In less than an hour everything was changed. Fired by her immediate charms, he burst all the bonds of etiquette and carried his bride off to his own tents. He made her his queen and put her like a seal upon his heart. For the child whom he had formerly married there was little thought, and the new bride, who for so many years had loved him from his portrait with a passionate eagerness, became the ruler as well as the loving servant of her prince.

The daily lives of these Rajput ladies of Mewár and Márwár may not have many deep interests but they are by no means empty. Among the greater chiefs, the woman's life is the usual life of palaces, with luxuries at command and with corresponding duties. There are servants to order and affairs to manage. Most ladies read and hear recitations; maid-servants sometimes sing; and children have to be cared for and tended. Sewing is a common amusement in which most Rajput women are expert. Occasionally a Rajput girl is heard of who, in the remoter districts, goes out riding or even shooting, dressed sometimes as a man, though seldom indeed can such amusements, in a caste which follows the seclusion of women, be entertained after childhood. There are, however, among advanced chiefs with modern ideas not a few instances in which there is a tennis-court in the palace grounds for the ladies, where the wives play together or with their husband and his nearest relations. And there are some rare States where even the semblance of seclusion is being discarded and the ladies drive abroad or shoot big game in the jungle.

These, however, are the liberties of the great. Among the lesser nobility, where riches are usually wanting and position has to be maintained by a stricter observance of traditional rule, the manner of life is busier, with less need of pleasure-seeking. In such a minor country-house, the wife will usually rise with the sun. If her mother-in-law is alive, she goes first to her room and wishes her a good morning. Then comes, what is in all such households a duty of first importance, the care of the dairy-farm with its noble white cows. The milk and whey is always distributed to servants and dependents by the lady herself. That done, she has a bath and says a short prayer for her husband, sees the children have their breakfast, and visits the kitchen. The proudest nobleman's wife would think shame of herself, if she did not superintend the cooking and at need take a hand in the baking of cakes and special delicacies. She sees to it that her husband and all male guests—usually numerous—have their breakfast before she herself eats her meal with her women. In that hot land, all sleep who can in the middle of the day, and the Rajput woman is no exception. When a couple of hours later she rises, she seeks for some amusement for the afternoon. All Rajput ladies are brought up from childhood to the strictest care of their persons and are taught even physical exercises. Before they are married they have learnt every device by which they can preserve or heighten their beauty and every art by which to sharpen their husbands' zest and devotion. For this purpose there are many things they learn which in Europe would be disapproved. But it is largely due to this care that they are faultlessly neat, fair, and attractive, and that so often their beauty lasts to advanced years. Thus in the quiet afternoon hours one of the frequent amusements is to inspect and brush clothes. Ladies keep large wooden chests, hasped and bolted with iron and often beautifully carved, very like the bridal chests of the Italian Renaissance. In them are stored the clothes in whose neatness and beauty they place their vanity. One by one they are taken out by the maid-servants and dusted and shown to the mistress and refolded and put back. It is a poor woman indeed who does not have at least fifteen to twenty skirts, from the cheaper cotton or red Turkey cloth to the richest silks and gold embroidery. Mantles (*Saris*) are at least as many and of bodices there may be forty or fifty. The maid-servants who fold the clothes are a notable institution. Rather household slaves than servants, born and bred in the house, and almost of pure Rajput blood themselves, they are the intimates of their mistress. One or two of them there will always be who have been her affectionate companions since childhood and have, on marriage, accompanied her to her new home. Such a girl is the lady's confidant and constant comrade, who looks to all her comforts, rubs her down after her bath and does skilful massage, knows all her secrets, brings her all rumours of the world, sleeps at her side in her husband's absence, and is her much cherished friend. Often, especially in youth, the two spend their afternoons sewing together. Amongst the Rajputs of Káthiawád, besides the pretty bodices that they often sew themselves, it is the custom for girls to embroider fringed strips of cloth for hanging across doors or squares to fasten upon walls for use as ornament at marriages and festivals. Little pieces of glass or mica are let into the embroidery and the patterns very much resemble those still sewn by peasant women in Hungary, whither they were also brought from the same tribal centres of Asia. Reading, visiting, chatting take up the rest of the day till evening approaches. Then the Rajput woman puts on her richer dresses and her jewelry and gets ready for dinner and the night.

RÁJPUT LADY FROM CUTCH

The Ladies of the Aristocracy

The Rajput women of Káthiawád and Cutch deserve some special mention, both for their beauty and their exceptional cleverness. Beautiful they are above all other women of India except only in Kashmir, fair with a rich fresh golden tint of skin, with full soft eyes, and with long black hair. In their apparel they are particularly tasteful, and the green hues that they specially affect set off their complexion at its best under the Indian sky. Of their intelligence there is no doubt, and throughout the Rajput country they are respected for their talents and perhaps, shall we add, feared for their intrigue. Jealous and ambitious to a fault, they are not ignorant even of the use of poison; and at least it is a proverb that "She marries the land, not the man." Gallant and courageous they are, even in evil, and it is not so long ago that the tale was told of a not-virtuous princess that night after night in the dark hours saddled a riding camel with her own hands in the stable and rode six miles out to join a lover, and before dawn, another six miles back, unseen, unknown, with the threat of a dagger-thrust, if discovered, always in her mind. But when well-beloved and cherished, these Rajput women are charming companions and faithful, assiduous helpmates.

Besides the tribes who can claim to be Rajputs of authentic origin, descended as was said from the Central Asian invaders who transformed ancient India to its present type, it follows reasonably enough from the constitution of the tribal entities and from the eternal facts of power and sovereignty, that there are many others who put forward a claim more or less substantiated to a similar recognition. Such are the slightly later invaders of similar strains who came to India from Scythia by a different road, the Jhadejas of Cutch and Káthiawád, for instance, with their frequent marriages with Mussulmans. These have at least a perfectly legitimate title to the name by a sort of cadet copyhold. The hill Rajputs of the Himalayas, among whom for generations survived the last indigenous school of Indian painting, can also fairly put forward a claim based on historical descent. But in addition, throughout Northern India, whenever by the fortune of circumstance a new tribe, not yet included as a caste in the orthodox Hindu system, has attained to princely power, the claim to true Rajput ancestry, for a time overlaid and obscured by the dust-layers of adversity, is propounded and defended. Minstrels in India are no less complacent than genealogists and heralds in Europe; and a ruling chief can have a mythical founder of his line disinterred from unknown records as readily as can a British peer. Instances are many and notorious; but it would be invidious to retail cases, where very often the tribe or its ruling family are in every way worthy of inclusion.

Among the Hindu aristocracy not yet fully recognized as Rajput, perhaps the most notable are the Mahrattas. Cultivators of the arid Deccan highlands, their swift-raiding horsemen carved out many a principality in the last three centuries. Several regiments

MAHRATTI LADY

of the Indian army are recruited from these stern and hardy tribes, and the Mahratta has fought steadily and well on the Euphrates and the Yser. Among the ruling chiefs, the generosity, loyalty, and gallantry of H.H. the Maharaja Scindia of Gwalior, in particular, have now become famous throughout the world.

Besides the ruling chiefs, the Mahratta tribes have a number of families of lesser nobility, above the mass of poorer farmers and peasants. Five of the tribes boast a purer birth and loftier ancestry; while in all ninety-nine tribes or branches of the race are counted. But in all tribes, far greater is the distinction between gentle and simple than among the Rajput clans. The Rajput clans form a real brotherhood in which, in many senses, each man is as good as another, wealth and power being accidentals only upon the leading strain. Over the whole social life is the tradition of the feudal fief and tenure, where all hold as gentlemen by their soldiers' service. Among the Mahrattas there has never been this history of feudal aristocracy. And even more perhaps, a certain democratic tendency and a certain proneness to claim "rights" in the true democratic spirit, make it natural for those who have attained nobility to distinguish themselves by a haughtier aloofness. In many ways this tendency has affected the Mahratta woman. It has introduced the *purdah* or seclusion for one thing among a people to whom it is not natural, first among the nobility, and now to a modified degree among the richer or prouder of the farmer class.

Among the mass it hardly exists even in name. More obvious still is the difference in appearance between the *lady* and the *woman*. The latter is like the generality of the Deccan population—one sect of Brahmans alone excepted—dark, stunted, hardly attractive. The former is fair, graceful, sometimes singularly charming. Seen at her best (and there are now not a few who in the disuse of seclusion in the more modern houses may be so seen) she is intelligent if quiet, winning though a trifle austere, grave and refined. The Mahratta lady lacks the open, ready smile and frank feminine fascination of the Rajput, but she has her own severer appeal. There is something in her always that is virginal. She goes through life as if unconscious of evil or at least as one deliberately and finely passing by with eyes unnoticing. Almost she reminds one of the girl-student resolute upon her way to lectures. Or—shall we say ?—in her is something of the Florentine school, in the Rajput princess the full rich bloom of Venice.

But in the Peninsula where it narrows to a cape against Ceylon there still survives an earlier segregated India, untouched, or almost so, by Scythian immigration. It never knew those tribal communities, now broken up and regrouped and again assimilated, which left behind as their living memorial the strenuous organism of the Rajput clans. In the south, where the green of the rice-fields gleams bright like emerald, and traffic moves slowly upon great waterways, a world survives, two thousand years old, fallen perhaps a little to decrepitude, of indigenous Dravidians—caste-ridden, they, from the first known times—and rarer immigrant Aryans. And in that world out of the teeming millions of the Dravidian population, akin perhaps in remote ages to the inhabitants of the South Seas, the nobility are the Nairs. Aristocracy they can hardly perhaps be called with propriety, since they themselves do not claim to rule as being best. Rather they derive their nobility, by their own showing, from the fact that they were deemed worthy by the Aryan priests, whom they acknowledge to be the highest of mankind. The Nairs are a community, rather than a caste or tribe, with powers of assimilation. A large infusion of Aryan blood, obtained from the favours of the priesthood whom they venerate, has given them a peculiar distinction from the Dravidian masses.

In the "Relations of the Most Famous Kingdom in the World," which was published in the year of Grace 1611 by Master Johnson, this southern nobility was abundantly described: "It is strange to see how ready the souldiour of this country is at his weapons: they are all gentile men and tearmed Naires. At seven years of age they are put to school to learn the use of their weapons, where, to make them nimble and active, their sinews and joints are stretched by skilful fellows and anointed with the oyle sesamus. By this anointing they become so light and nimble that they will wind and turn their bodies as if they had no bones, casting them forward, backward, high and low, even to the astonishment of the beholders. Their continual delight is in their weapon, persuading themselves that no nation goeth beyond them in skill and dexterity." They are no longer warriors and the only soldiers of Nair caste are the household brigade maintained by H.H. the Maharaja of Travancore. But they are still brave, and in their play the sword and buckler and the bow and arrow keep their place.

Nowadays it is the women who have won the higher fame. Seldom in any country can there have been a womanhood that has received such universal eulogy. From the earliest histories of Malabar to the latest writings of French tourists, the chorus of praise has been a monody. Old Duarte Barbosa, writing centuries ago his "Description of the Coasts of East Africa and Malabar," already clothed his impression in admiring words. Most of all he notes that "they are very clean and well-dressed women and they hold it a great honour to know how to please men." This careful cleanliness and a certain grave sort of neatness are indeed recurrent in every description. The bath is to them a very article of faith and they bathe not daily but, almost it might be said, hourly. Beside each house is a large private tank or pond of masonry with broad stone steps leading to the water, and there are few moments in the hot daylight hours when it does not resound to a woman's laugh. They use the nuts of various saponaceous plants to free hair and skin from the slightest impurity; and no robe, however slightly soiled, is ever worn again till it is thoroughly

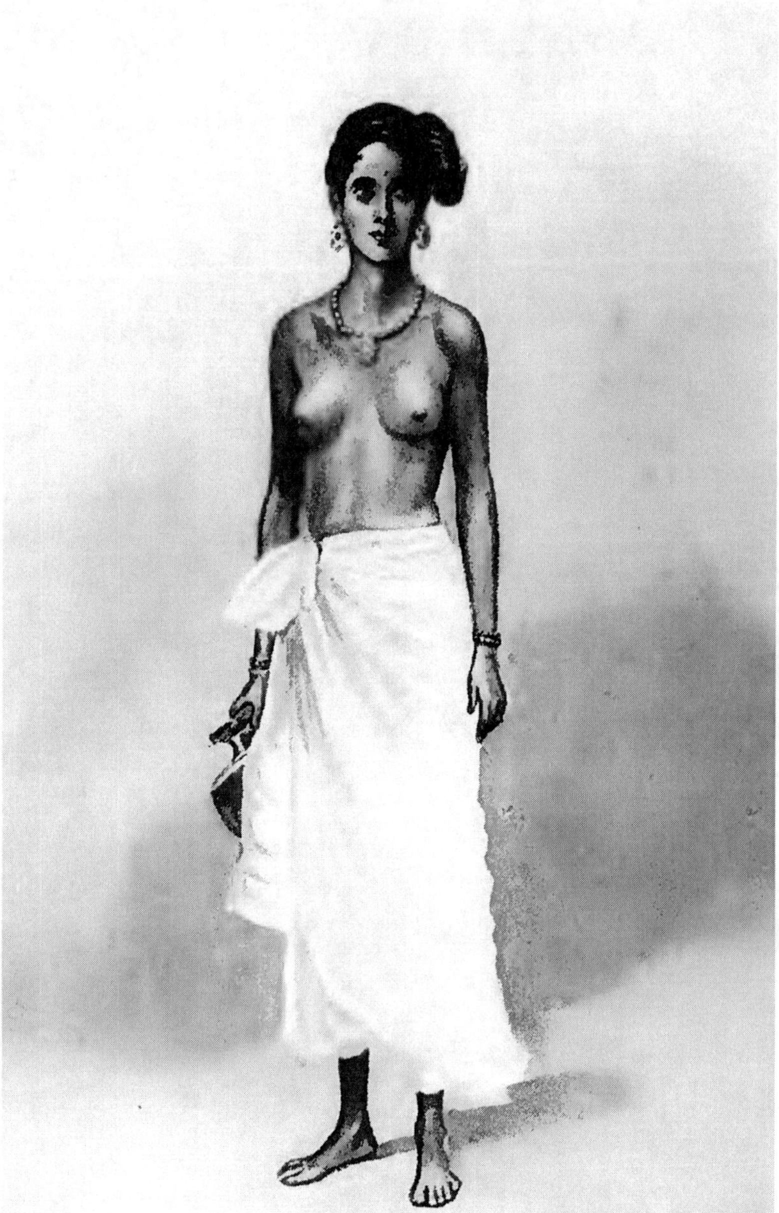

NAIR LADY

cleaned by the washerwoman. A scrupulous cleanliness and a fastidious neatness—a total impression of almost hieratic purity—this exhales from the Nair woman like an emanation. By their grave simplicity an English official was inspired to a pretty compliment, as he toiled through some red-tape Census Report with much talk of "excess of females" in the Nair population. "They could never be accused," he reported with mock indignation, "of an 'excess of females.' The most beautiful women in India, if numerous, could never be excessive."

The general picture of grave and simple purity is heightened by the appearance of their houses, each aloof and separate with a certain quiet dignity in its own grounds. A bathing tank and a garden, these are the first conditions of every household; and the garden is luxuriant with the great rough stems of the jack-fruit tree, the graceful areca and cocoa-nut palms, and bright green, broad-leaved banana plants. To the east is the gate, through the garden, to the house, with a stile to cross and a gate-house or lodge at its side. The house itself, with its large household all related through the female line, has on the ground floor its kitchen and store-rooms, an open courtyard, and a large dining-hall. And above, with two separate staircases, lie on one side the women's, on the other the apartments of the men, segregated entirely one from another. In such houses with all their numerous family-members, brothers and sisters and cousins and aunts and children always growing up, a certain quiet discipline and an instinctive order, from being a duty, becomes a constant habit. Comfort and tranquillity, if they are to be had, exact self-effacing restraint and gentle deference to others' wishes and requirements. Whatever is boisterous and impulsive, the self-assertive and the crude, has had to be effaced and smoothed away, as pebbles shaken together in a bag lose their sharp edges. The manners that result are quiet and self-contained, a little solemn perhaps, as of people traversing a cathedral, but sweetened by human charity and a pleasant touch of worldly irony.

The dress is simple in the extreme, a single white cloth that reaches from the waist to the knee. This for long ages has been the sole honoured dress of the Nair lady, above all fear as she is and above reproach. That in all public places she should go boldly and unashamed, with no self-conscious daring, but simply and modestly, with the upper part of her body uncovered before all men, has been the law of her community. Only jewelry she wears, a gold or silver chain, even a gold belt about her waist, gold bosses in her ears, and a necklace whose pendants are as the cobra's hood upon her neck. Sometimes, however, especially in these later days, and when she travels to other provinces, she throws a cloth over her shoulders and bosom, with a certain shyness, as of something coquettish and immodest.

Amusements too are simple, but to their thinking plentiful and quietly enjoyable. All girls are taught to read and write, and not a few are highly educated.

They are in general on the happiest terms with their husbands, whom they do not see too much and whose affections are not blunted by the daily usage of a common household and the dulling minutiæ of daily life. When, however, there is incompatibility, they separate simply and naturally without unkindness to seek a better loved mate. In leisure hours, swinging, two or three merry girls on the same swing, is a favourite amusement, and singing and dancing are often enjoyed, especially at the great autumn festival when the house is filled with presents and each one gives every one else a yellow cloth or a toy or an ornament. Prettiest of all their amusements, however, and most symbolic of all that quiet, so sweetly singular life on the backwaters of the south, is that of flower-decoration. In the early morning the children of the large household go into the fields to gather flowers and bring them back in armfuls. Then all sit down in the courtyard, and with their gathered blossoms make bright decorative patterns on the walls and floor. Best loved of all is a flower-carpet over which they raise a booth, gaily festooned with other flowers. When all is complete, the neighbours are asked to come in and admire; and they compare it with their own in turn. But the finest flowers of all are the sweet gravely tender women of Malabar.

When he turns to the Mussulman aristocracy of India, the European finds himself on ground more familiar, as it is more similar to the landscape of his own social existence. These chiefs and nobles are the descendants—in most part—of soldier adventurers who, as generals or as governors under the Emperors of Delhi, or as rebels and fighters for their own hand, achieved estates and even principalities. They have no caste or tribe to distinguish them from their fellows, but owe their position to their authority and landed interest. As sons of Adam, they hold, all men are in essence equal, but Destiny has apportioned sovereignty to one and to another beggary. They rise and fall, as in Europe, too, heritages are wasted and fortunes won ; and they rely upon no mystic ordinance and no hieratic ceremonial for their prestige. The frank acceptance of the world as it is, *facts* alone one would say having importance, makes the Mussulman gentleman and his family appear figures fully human and comprehensible. Polygamy and the seclusion of women alone cause disparities, superficial even these in many respects.

The permission to marry up to four wives is in practice seldom utilized. The commandment to treat all wives alike, with equal favour and cherishing, in itself makes righteous polygamy by no means easy. But a more actual obstacle is the natural jealousy of the woman and her great influence. There are few Mussulman ladies whose husbands are not just the least thing " henpecked." And few of them will allow a rival to enter the zanána without a struggle. Only in a few of the most powerful courts is it prevalent to any conspicuous degree ; and in such royal households where it exists, it flies often in the face of Holy Scripture no less than human sense and comfort. It is then

MUSSULMAN LADY OF NORTHERN INDIA

a vice and not an observance. Seclusion—the "purdah"—exists with a severity far exceeding modern Turkey or even Egypt, and still more in excess of the Prophet's teaching; but it falls short of the unreasoning stringency of the Rajput code. It is relaxed for one thing by the recognition in each case of certain persons who stand "within the enclosure," as it is called, or in other words are free to meet the women of the house unveiled. In this circle are included a large number of male relatives and even, in a few cases, the husband's most intimate friends, as well as servants brought up from childhood within the family. Moreover, the restriction becomes less oppressive when it is relieved by the wide freedom to visit women-friends which is generally sanctioned. Veiled though they drive through the streets and unseen, there are few things which are not noted by the keen eyes behind the peep-holes in the shrouding cloak.

The Mussulman girl of the better class is in early childhood taught to recite prayers and to read the Qor'an in Arabic, though without understanding of the words she reads. As she grows older she is usually taught more, and attains a fair knowledge of Urdu, while, if she shows signs of greater capacity, she will often learn Persian as well. To read simple books in Urdu and Persian is at least a common accomplishment, and there are not a few who can themselves read or, at least, understand the elegant odes of Hafiz. In household management and the care of her children the Mussulman lady is able to find incessant occupation, while there is no one who more appreciates the pleasures of a garden with runnels of flowing water under a tropic sky. She rises very early, and shortly after dawn she is to be found among the roses in the walled garden. Chess and backgammon are frequent amusements. In talismans, omens, charms and the evil eye she has an unshakable belief, which survives every trial. And in her later years she looks forward to the sacred pilgrimage to Mecca, with all its difficulties and hardships, as the last and best employment of a well-spent life. Something there is truly noble in that figure of an old lady, veiled in white, facing, after a long life behind the curtain, the crowded port, the steamer, and the desert Bedouins. But sweetest picture of all in the womanhood of the Mussulman nobility is the growing girl, not yet a woman, in coloured silk trousers, long robe, or shirt of fine Dacca muslin, and velvet cap gold-embroidered, as she sits cross-legged beneath a shady tree and recites aloud from the silk-covered Qor'an that is open before her on its carved sandalwood rest.

The Middle Classes

"Things never changed since the time of the Gods,
The flowing of water, the way of love."

Japanese Song. LAFCADIO HEARN.

FROM BURMAH

Chapter V

THE MIDDLE CLASSES

In a vast empire with a population of over three hundred millions, in area a continent, with some thirty-five main languages and of dialects none can say how many, with different religions and with cultures divided from each other by centuries of progress, anything like an adequate description of the middle-class woman would be a task beyond human power, and its perusal beyond the patience of the most enduring reader. Less difficult by far would it be to head a chapter "The middle classes of Europe," and, within its limits, after running from Greece and Roumania to Spain and England, to scale the heights upon which, like an inspiration, the womanhood of France sits enthroned. But there are at least some essentials in which the womanhood of the Indian middle classes becomes congruous, differing therein from the women of other countries, Europe for instance, or America or China. Perhaps it may be tried by the selection of a few types, with the aid of contrast and analysis, in some way to express their essential atmosphere and habit.

Burmah must, one finds, go to the wall, not most certainly for any fault of its own but because it lies so far apart from the total of Indian life. For administration it is placed within the confines of the Indian Empire, but with the Indian peoples its people has no lot or part. To omit it seems almost a pity, so frankly independent are its women and so fascinating—free above the women of most nations and consonant to an unusual degree with ultimate human ideals. One sees such a little Burmese lady sometimes, but how rarely, in India, the wife perhaps of some English officer or of a high Burmese councillor, so a picture may stand as reminder of smiling daintiness, like some porcelain figurine glazed and tinted in the furnace of human freedom.

In India proper, of the middle classes, the most important, and perhaps the most enigmatic, figure is the Brahman's. The class is certainly an aristocracy in one, the etymological, sense. For it is as being best that they hold power and the power that they hold is, even to this day, most undeniable. Aristocracy—" rule of the best "—of those rather who are admitted to be best—if this be indeed a meaning true to fact, then the Brahmans should be included in or alone comprise that rank. With many of them their very appearance, their gait and self-composure, support the rôle. With steady untroubled eye, straight nose and sensitive nostril, fair skin, " pride in their port " and self-restraint in every gesture, they move through the mass of common men, as if conscious of a higher mission. By the sacred thread across the shoulder they proclaim themselves twice-born, once from a mortal womb and once again at an auspicious hour in childhood by initiation to the sacred mysteries. Calm and indifferent, serene with a careful precision and habit of restraint, they incarnate in their manner something of absolute repose, as if untouched by the mundane ebb and flow. Withal they are not in any customary sense a nobility. Perhaps, it may be said, they have transcended even nobility. In any case the proudest noble must at times, and some must constantly, admit the ascendancy, spiritual though it be, of these born preceptors. The greatest ruler will eat food cooked by the poorest Brahman beggar; but no Brahman, desperate with the pangs of destitution, would accept even a glass of water from a monarch's jug, the mere touch being a profanation to the nutriment of sanctity. In Southern India, where the Brahman, immigrant from Aryan races, was most successful in exploiting the indigenous population by the means of religious awe, the Nair nobility are abject in their recognition of this hierarchic superiority. In every word of speech the Nair throws himself, as a clod of mud, before the Brahman's feet to be trampled and contemned. His house becomes, in speaking to a Brahman, his poor dunghill and the Brahman's house his palace; his teeth are dirty in his speech, and the Brahman's pearls; his sleep is a mere falling into snores, and the Brahman's an honourable slumber.

But in ordinary speech, in Europe and no less in India, the concept of nobility or aristocracy in its worldly relations implies other qualities. A certain tinge of feudal tradition colours our thought; and a nobleman is always conceived primarily as a fighter and a leader of his own men in his own estate. Love of sport, a certain careless gaiety, an eupeptic cheerfulness and a happy enjoyment, face to face with a world in which nothing really matters, coupled with the readiness to do the duties of his station and to die for honour, these are qualities that make up the mental picture.

It is not to such a class that the Brahman belongs. To life and the pleasures of life, he stands as a pillar of negation. Not here and now one conceives him beckoning, but in a reality transcending all appearance in duty and existence. Privation is for him the highest rule and participation in the world is at most an inexorable concession to accidental forces. The Brahman's life must, in semblance at least, be one of constant abstention, rigidly guarded. The show of enjoyment and the joy of healthy natural life must be repressed or at least veiled discreetly. Between him and mere sensual humanity he has dug a gulf, impassable.

Of Brahmans only a few are by ordination priests. The majority fill the professional classes, as administrators, clerks, astrologers, scholars, physicians, lawyers, and the like. Some are money-lenders and not a few are cultivators of the soil. There are even rare Brahman houses which, in spite of religious prohibition, have usurped the thrones of princes. But in all there exists not only a sense of solidarity as being

LADY FROM MYSORE

sanctified, but also this ideal of abstention, leading in practice not unseldom to a grave and measured hypocrisy. As a whole they are the professional class of India, they and the rival caste, the Kayasthas or "scribes," and maintain with admirable earnestness the tastes and pursuits of an intellectual, idealizing, and temperate order. Mental discipline, the suppression of the impulsive act, a habit of restriction so incessant as to become almost instinctive, these they have to a degree almost overwhelming.

Among Rajput women one finds certainly the highest development of the individual with the greatest charm and the fullest humanity, and it is they, almost alone, who have achieved the heroic. But to India as a whole the ordinary ideal of woman in her relation to social function is represented by the more reticent figure of the Brahman. She is woman as in his life the ordinary man would wish to find her, quiet, devoted, managing and pious.

Nowhere is the Brahman woman so true to the type presented in this ideal as in the Madras Presidency and in the Bombay Deccan. And never is she so true to herself as when she goes, sedately, to the temple. In her hand she carries the brass tray on which she has put her humble offerings of ochre powder and flowers with a wick burning beside them ; and she goes looking neither to the right nor to the left. She rings the bell which summons the God's attention to his worshipper and walks the prescribed ceremonial steps round the idol with a grave unquestioning dignity. And her whole life is one unceasing round of service, in which humility is elevated by an ever-present sense of Divine ordinance. To the lowly in heart she feels—almost one might say she knows, so strongly does she feel—belongs the kingdom of heaven. In service to find fulfilment, even happiness, that is her God-given mission. She grinds corn and cooks, carries water and washes the house, nurses her children, waits upon her family, as also she draws ornamental patterns with white and red chalks upon her door-step, all with a humble pride and joy in the singleness of her devotion. In poorer houses, in the houses of far the greater number of her class, she is at work all day from long before the first dawning till at last at night she falls into the deep slumbers of exhaustion. There are few who keep servants, except for an occasional old woman who comes to help with the rougher tasks. And in addition to the household labour, she is forced, too early, to premature childbirth, and protracted nursing. For charm and coquetry, for all the arts by which woman gladdens life and creates a liberal society, she has, if she had the inclination, no spare time or energy. She ages early, spent by exhausting labour and the recurring burden of unregulated childbirth, unwarmed by joy, unlit by passion.

But the bare life of poverty and unending labour is illumined by a spiritual exaltation. With the performance of their service the million Saint Theresas of the Deccan are able to find within their hearts a satisfying happiness. Like nuns, by an austere self-repres-

A SOUTHERN INDIAN TYPE

sion, they avert their eyes from humanity and the human purposes of life; and when they are forced to see, they persuade themselves to despise. They live as it were in a spiritual cloister. But even in this world they are not altogether without reward, though it comes late in life. The love and devoted kindness of her sons, that is the one constant meed of service upon which the woman counts. And there are few things more impressive than an Indian son's look when he turns to his mother or the tone in which, even years after her death, he speaks of his childhood at her side. And in old age when she in turn, with her husband, succeeds to the management of the large joint family household, she finds a peaceful joy in the ordering of their simple life and the caresses of her clustering grandchildren. At the end, when death lays her to sleep at last, she dies in the hope of an untroubled peace, as one who has accomplished a lengthy service not without pain and effort.

Such perhaps most truly are the women of India, as through a large continent the greatest number of its inhabitants would like to see them. Not for this world, they might say, is the labour; not for love and enjoyment and greater power and finer emotions and self-development and the glories of nature do they thirst. Of the fervours of youth and the vivid joys of mere active BEING, of the fine harmonies between soul and sense in expanding, self-perfecting human functions, of a humanity that should be self-sufficient, free in the face of the eternal universe and glad in the fight for mastery with obstructive matter, they have not even a conception. To an Indian Antigone no chorus would sing of human power and magnitude. Only the preacher would instruct in humility and abnegation.

Even the richest Brahman women of the South spend their leisure hours in a manner that accords with the common ideal. Relieved of the more exhausting house-work by the labour of the servants, they spend the afternoon hours when they are at rest in the reading of the Purans, those grosser Scriptures or, one might perhaps with truer comparison say, those Hagiologies in which priests have deformed the too subtle tenets of Hindu theosophy with the flesh of mythology. In the reciting of these legends, and in lengthy prayers and ritual performance the wealthy Brahman lady is content to find the entertainment of her leisure.

The same ideal of service and privation is to be found no less in Bengal, sweetened however and softened like the more languid air. There is something hard, even cruel perhaps, in the arid Deccan plain with its burning dry winds and its stony hill-sides, and its stern, thrifty, self-centred people. Its asceticism is harsh and rough, the sour ferment as it were of crude souls in fear of a fierce Deity, looking by abnegation to secure the grace that alone can give salvation. The spirit is that, almost, of a Hindu Calvinism, savagely abnegatory. A softer piety, as of some Italian nunnery among roses and olive trees over the blue sea, inspires the womanhood of Bengal. They have a devotion no less intense, their service and self-sacrifice is no smaller ; but they are filled also with the pity that assuages and the love

BENGALI LADY

that makes things sweet. To be kind and tender in a world which, with all its evil and pain, is pervaded by a loving and merciful Providence, such is the spirit in which they render service. The large houses of Bengal, embowered in trees, have a claustral peace as well as labour. The lives of the women in them are coloured by the tender light of pity and affection. Often in the warm nights under the star-strewn sky, young girls creep to each other and whisper little gaieties.

In general, among the middle classes of Bengal, women practise a seclusion that is, however, not too rigid. It is a seclusion like that of classic Athens, not savagely jealous as it still is in many Rajput houses. But with the renaissance that in the last fifty years has so greatly altered life in this great province, many have learnt to discard orthodoxy and with it the traditional restrictions. At Benares, especially, many a Bengali lady can be seen walking openly to the temples and the sacred river. Always she bears a perfect courtesy and a rounded balanced dignity. Of the newer school, too many perhaps have aspirations gleaned from the lighter English novels which they eagerly read—dreams for whose passage the ivory gates of Hinduism were never meant to open. But deep in the hearts of all—far deeper than such fashions —are the images of Sita and Sakuntala. Some play tennis and ride, some there are who return from English schools and the smarter section of London society with the gossip of Ranelagh or the bridge club and a wider taste for amusement. But there are none who discard the tenderness and soft devotion of their native womanhood. Nowhere in India have there been so many marriages between English and Indian; nowhere have they been more successful. The number of women really educated, appreciative of art and literature, a few even themselves poets and writers, is out of all comparison large; and the artistic rebirth in Bengal must to some extent have been shaped by the influence of women's grace on the social world. Without departing from the prescribed fields of service and abnegation, they take their part in every important movement—sometimes perhaps unwisely! But at times they have brought untold benefit by their acts. So a few years ago did the brave girl who by the sacrifice of her own life slew a great social evil—the purchase of men at the price of ruinous dowries. It must at least be conceded that the women of Bengal, descendant from mixed races but long since truly Indian, have clothed the sacerdotal ideal in vestment of soft and womanly grace.

But there are other parts of India where even the Brahman woman has diverged from this ideal, or—should one not rather say?—has transfused into it the feelings and robust sensuality of a more vigorous nature. Where the late conquerors from the North have settled, where rich plains bear wheat and millet, and fields are hedged with the milk-bush and the cactus, where the great trees make the country seem like an English park, and the air bites cold in the winter mornings when a skin of ice crackles on road-side pools, where in the hot months the sun hangs like

A NÁGAR BEAUTY

a disc of brass over the panting earth, there the pulse beats stronger and a larger nature sways the will. Women there have their claims as well as duties; and from life they demand, besides the right to serve, a broader power also and a rich fulfilment. They wish for love and to be loved, and even in their service they aspire to govern. For their womanhood they claim at least some freedom. The texts are still the same; but they are commented by a bolder temperament. The distinction holds good perhaps for all the women of real Hindustan—for the lusty graceful women of Allahabad, for instance, and the upper Ganges Valley.

But nowhere can this fine and active type be better studied than in the Nágar caste of Káthiawád and Gujarát. The Nágar community came to India with the last Scythian hordes; and almost at once, at the great fire baptism of Ajmer, attained the rank of Brahmans. To this day, so high do they hold themselves above all others, they hardly trouble to use the title Brahman, but call themselves merely Nágar, with a proud simplicity, as who would say, "I am the Prince." For centuries they have held the appointments of the State and been famous as administrators. They are to be found in every rank and in every department of the public services, clever, courteous, receptive, and self-confident. Their pride has become a byword among other castes; and their success has made them the mark of envy and dislike. But there can be no question of the ability with which they have held their position, nor of the keen, progressive intellect that guides their interests and activities. They have an eager humanity, and a keen understanding of worldly good and evil, and are above the hypocritical renunciations and pessimistic sanctity of a priestly class. Literature they hold in honour; and the creative instinct, which leads many of them to administration as the career in which man expresses his active will through the minds and morals of mankind, forces others of their community to self-expression in thought and language. If renunciation there be, it is here, not for a mere negation, in itself fruitless; but to the end of a greater realization in the material given by humanity. In this dynamic will, the women have a proportional share. Ambitious and intellectual, they partake in the interests of their families and encourage or advise their husbands and their children. For the achievement of purpose they are ready for every sacrifice; but the consciousness of larger interests ennobles the sacrifice as it humanizes the purpose. They too serve, as every Hindu woman seeks to serve, and the Nágar wife, like her sisters, will cook and wash and stand aside before her man and wait upon his meals. But her devotion is shaped by a less trammelled intellect, and she claims in return an immediate recompense of love and attention.

Very beautiful are the Nágar women, and their beauty is the theme of countless songs and ballads. Fair with a rich golden vivid fairness, like the colour of ripe wheat, with dark eyes in whose depth glows a spark of passion and round which humour and laughter play, with full petulant lips, figures finely rounded and firmly plump like the quail, with graceful movement and slender limb, the whole lit up by intelligence and comprehension and a touch of conscious charm, the Nágar woman presents a picture that remains unforgotten. Even laborious study seems to have no power to rob her of her looks, and the girl-graduate is fresh and graceful, as if she had never bent over Euclid or deductive logic. One meets them so at times in Ahmedabad or Baroda, in the houses of the highest officials, clever, well-read, well-bred, with perfect manners and astounding beauty, like some memory of the Italian Renaissance, taking no small part in the establishment of an urbane and liberal society, and like the *donne* of Boccacio they return to their homes to serve and cherish their husbands. And of love they can repeat the whole gamut. Indeed, the keynotes of this society, with all its undertones of Hindu abnegation—as in Florence, too, one imagines an undercurrent, not too discordant, from Savonarola's denunciations—are not unlike Italy in the great age. Women have similar duties with a touch of the same implied seclusion ; they have the same intrigues and stolen pleasures, the same essentially natural poise in life ; they are now even beginning a similar application to learning and poetry. And of love too they have no lesser lore and experience than those ladies who, finely natural and fittingly acquiescent in their sex, gladdened and made illustrious the Courts of Mantua and Ferrara.

Even more beautiful than the women in the Nágar caste are their charming and delightful children.

With the round oval of their faces, the fair bloom of their skins, the growing intelligence that dances in their eyes, they at once captivate all who look. In general up to the age of eight or ten they remain naked (though an unfortunate new fashion, imitated from customs made necessary by the cold grey skies of England, tends to hamper their free beauty in ugly and unwholesome clothes), and the light movement of frail gold-browned limbs in the Indian air is sheer refreshment to the eye.

Devotion, then, the Nágar woman certainly stands for, devotion and the due and harmonious fulfilment of the duties of her station. A woman she is always, fully and truly womanly. But she is far above the mere privative of empty abnegation. Beauty she knows and values, and she is not ignorant or afraid of the power that kindly beauty can exercise in the affairs of men. Learning she can recognize and honour ; literature she assists ; even of art, she is not, like her sisters, much afraid. In Gujarát from of old the dainty custom has remained by which on certain festivals, the feast of lamps for instance, ladies of the highest classes meet in the open streets of the residential quarters and chant choral songs while they move round in a circle, beating time with their hands and bending gracefully up and down. They sing of spring and flowers and the sports of girl-friends in palace-gardens. But in the large industrial cities which in the last generation have risen upon the older towns with their restricted social circles, the publicity of the streets has become inconvenient. The Nágar ladies in Ahmedabad, for instance, have taken a leading part in transferring the old songs to larger concert halls in clubs and similar places, and at the same time raising the standard and artistic value of the performance. Those who have ever heard such a concert must be grateful for a movement full at the same time of beauty and colour and sweet sound along with modesty and perfect taste. For a higher social life, with heightened enjoyments and a rational freedom, for self-development and wider interests, yet well within the limits that nature prescribes for woman, distinct from the far other limits set to man by his divergent functions, for a life that has in it something of Greece as well as the main ideals of Hinduism, the Nágar woman, for all the illiberal asceticism of the Brahman tradition, may emphatically stand.

In the mercantile classes the same ideals persist, deflected however by the incidents of their livelihood and to an even greater extent by a profound difference in spiritual aspect. Of the Hindu trading classes by far the most important and the most ubiquitous are the merchants of Márwár, of Gujarát, and of Cutch. All follow one of two sects, the Vaishnava or the Jain —the latter in essence a different religion, originally indeed a protest against Hinduism but now little more than a sect, another ripple, so to say, on the waters of national faith. Both at any rate are protests against Brahman orthodoxy and the gnostic philosophies of essential Hinduism. Numerically and in its effects, by far the more important is Vaishnavism. In the form in which it has been adopted by the trading classes, it is the belief that by love alone can God be realized. It centres upon Krishna, that tender and sportive figure, in whom the God Vishnu again came to earthly life, and in whom are enshrined the memories of a once-living hero. On Him mythology and popular song have lavished their softest endearments and their most entrancing images. In His name have been composed the voluptuous love-poems of many generations; and the dalliances of Krishna with the milk-maids and His beloved Radha are the constant theme to which Indian passion turns for lyrical expression. They are the familiar accompaniment in childhood as in age of the merchant's women-folk. In Vaishnavism such as this the devotee throws himself, as a suppliant, on God's grace and love alone. He acknowledges indeed his innate incapacity to apprehend the Godhead, but he aspires at least to feel something of His Glory in those ecstasies of self-abandonment which can be likened on this earth only to the passionate love of man and woman. In their prayers too they associate with the God that consort Lakshmi or Rukhmini, who gives wealth and prosperity—the benign divinity who with her lord preserves and maintains all living things and in loving-kindness intercedes for all who seek by love and submission to realize the Divine in the universe, be their sins manifold as the sands upon the shore.

In every land, of course, the pursuit of wealth as such must be opposed to higher spiritual activities and loftier aspirations. For the merchant the end must be the acquisition of riches for its own sake. All other purposes are either means or incidents. He must treat men and women as means and not as ends in themselves. He can have for humanity none of that respect which is felt by him who, as equal among equals, seeks as his end human perfection, or even by him who, again one of many equals, works, as he thinks, by pain and self-denial for the greater glory of God. Where acquisition is the supreme good, all else must be subordinate. And the methods of acquisition are really two-fold, either by careful saving and the starving of desire to accumulate useless metal tokens which are the equivalents of untasted pleasures, or by wilder speculation quickly to capture the wealth which, exchanged, can buy luxury and material gratification. Side by side, in the same class of men, the two methods can be seen. Extravagant abstention and extravagant lavishness, a fulfilment that is material or an abstention that is no less material, these in all countries are the marks of the merchant class. But they can be mitigated in their effect, as they were in the Italian Renaissance by the almost superstitious devotion of all ranks to the newly-exhumed classic ideal. In India this mitigation is given by the creed of Krishna and of love. Materialized though it has to be when refracted through the mind of man the acquisitive, it is still an influence, nicely attuned to the receiver, for something finer and ennobling. What there is of good, charity and spiritual significance in the merchant's life (and it is after all much) is mainly drawn from a faith which, even when interpreted in a too material sense, could hardly be replaced for its worshippers by any other *credo*. In modern Europe the aristocratic ideal has for the richer merchant something of the same significance and mitigating value. But for those outside the circle in which this ideal can be operative there is no other thought to raise and enlarge the spirit.

It is not difficult to see how all these influences must react upon the woman's life. The effects are further complicated by the fact that child-marriages are still the rule, and that only too often, in a trading class, the young bride is sold by her parents for large sums to an aged bridegroom. Among the larger number of the class, probably, acquisition is sought by rigid economy. The young wife finds herself stinted, therefore, of every comfort and even of the dresses and ornaments that by nature every woman desires. The husband holds the purse and makes almost all purchases himself. A few rupees only can reach the wife, and for these she has to account. Even if her husband is young, long hours in the shop, constant poring over account books, and little exercise only too soon make him obese and feeble. The only real interests are house-work, in which she has no final voice, and frequent, often ill-natured, gossip. On the other hand, she has this of advantage that her men-folk, weighing the world as they do by its material fruits, ascribe to women the first place in their pleasures. She is, therefore, in spite of all, able sometimes to

JAIN NUN

attain a real power that is discordant with her ostensible position. The passion is for the sex in general, not for the individual woman ; for a mere satisfaction of sense, not for a spiritual individualized love of the fitting mate. But a shrewd woman can play upon the passion and make it serve her own purposes. And when the trader's wife does manage to attain such influence, she uses it unsparingly for her own satisfaction. Many a comedy of manners is played, unseen, on the dark stage of the merchant's house. There are not a few husbands who, whether from love of gain or from sheer terror of their wives, shut their eyes complaisantly to divagations damaging to their honour. The practice common to many money-lenders of keeping burly Mussulman, often Afghan, servants in their households, is anything except an incentive to female virtue.

Among the merchants who follow the Jain religion, however, these conditions apply with less force. Their life is simpler and the imagination is unheated by the constant thought of loving ecstasy. The Jain *sadhvis*, a class of nuns recruited both from the unmarried and the widowed, bear a character that is far above reproach. With shaven heads and in yellow garments, a little square of cloth usually tied upon their lips to save them from inhaling the smallest insect, they wander through the country, begging and singing hymns, nowhere to remain above four days, leading a life of austerity for the glory of the spirit. They are irreproachable like Sisters of Mercy, and like Sisters of Mercy they can move safely among the roughest crowds, protected by the respect of all. Something of their simple and humble piety has penetrated to all ranks among the Jains; and the ladies of the Jain millionaires of Ahmedabad, owners of large cotton factories and masters of men and money, live their simple lives in the midst of riches with purity and quiet modesty.

Amongst the richest of the merchant class are the Bhatias, who gain rather by daring speculation than by niggardly effort. On the race-course, as in the exchange and cotton market, they are conspicuous figures, with a certain pleasing *bonhomie* and easy good-fellowship. The Bhatia women play a part in the social life of modern India that is hardly less conspicuous. Orthodox in the extreme, they are strict followers not of the ascetic but of the more human sect. They are able, therefore, to be strict in observance and orthodox in belief without abdicating the rights and enjoyments of humanity. They attend diligently to religious services and in the early hours of the morning the ways that lead to the Krishna temple are thronged with their carriages. To the High-priests, in whom they see the divinity incarnate, they give an adoration that is almost boundless. But, with all this, they claim from life the fulfilment of their humanity and their womanhood. Moreover, they demand something of excitement and palpitant emotion. A few there are who, like their men-folk, gamble, and there is none who will deny herself the excitement of jewelry and fine clothes, diaphanous fabrics half disclosing the limbs they cover. The

BHATIA LADY

worst offshoot of their orthodoxy is the practice of infant marriage; and there are few sections of the community in which young girls are so often married to old men, the parents profiting by the bride-price. As the remarriage of widows is forbidden, it follows necessarily that in the Bhatia caste there is a number, quite excessive, of young widows, in the first bloom of fresh maturity, often left with great fortunes. Fortunately for society, these widows, so numerous are they and the conditions of their marriage so manifestly unfair, have been able collectively to repudiate the hardships that enmesh the orthodox Brahman who has lost her husband. Among the Bhatias, there are few shaven heads! Neat and well dressed, with pleasing face and figure, perhaps too consciously demure, they strike an attractive note in the complex harmonies of modern India. The system by which they are married is hardly elevating and is opposed not only to the ideals but also to the commandments of the sacred texts; but a commercial class cannot get away from its own limitations. It is at least a great deal gained that it should be alleviated by a sensible appreciation of life and joy and by a degree of freedom which, though not of the highest and inmost kind, is more humanizing and liberal than the negatives of material self-denial. Self-control, control, that is, of and by the inner self in harmony with ultimate nature, is no doubt the concomitant of the highest liberty; but any liberty, even any licence, is better than the denial of the actual living self.

In the rich province of Gujarát, the home of so large a proportion of the merchants of India, there is a festival which embodies in its observance much of the inner feeling of the Indian woman. During the rains, for one waxing moon, the days are sacred to that Goddess, who represents the all-pervading energy of nature, the spouse of Shiva, the Great God, the ultimate Destroyer. During these days the maidens of middle-class Gujarát worship the Goddess with an eye fixed upon the attainment of the perfect husband. The little girls go in groups and bathe and pray, and they make the vow that is the Vow of Life. They may be as young as six or seven or eight, but year after year they renew the vow till they are married. Throughout the day they have to sit in a darkened room, reflecting upon the Goddess and upon the supreme boon of a good husband, but at times resting their minds by nursery tales or songs or innocent games with cards and dice. Then every morning they bathe again in the pond or river, where rival groups of girls make jokes upon each other and laugh and play. The many songs are the most touching part of the whole festival. And these songs represent a marriage of free choice, in which the girl chooses a husband from her suitors. How different from the present practice! Year after year, till they are married, they sing these songs. And who shall say how far this dream of choice may remain to mould their actions, even after the forced marriage that awaits them? The need of marriage at least, its

KHOJA LADY IN BOMBAY

supreme value to a woman's life, that is always before their eyes from early childhood ; and marriage is bound up with religion, with the personal gifts of the divine and happy wife of the Greatest God. But in the very songs, sanctioned by the goddess, the cry is always for the chosen mate, the giver of love and happiness. Little wonder if at times the grown girl, now become conscious, learns to know the difference between the husband selected under social conventions by her parents for his worldly circumstance and the man who, unsuitable perhaps in wealth or temperament, is yet nature-chosen to be the mate of her desires and the beloved of her heart. For the parents' choice is not always wise, and among sinful mankind there are not a few who will sacrifice a daughter's welfare to their own profit.

Of the Mussulman middle classes, the most conspicuous are the Bohras and the Khojas. Both belong to different branches of the Shiah sect, that sect which is to Islam what the Catholic Church is to Christianity. Both also are the descendants of Hindu communities which were converted in fairly recent times to the faith of salvation. Among the Khojas, especially, many Hindu customs have survived, and their law of succession in particular is not the law of the Qor'an but the survival of Hindu tribal custom. At this moment, perhaps, theirs is the most interesting of these communities, both because by their practical talents they have obtained a place of political leading among Indian Mussulmans and because they are—

with the exception of a small reforming branch—the religious followers of H.H. the Agha Khan, a prince so nobly known by his loyal efforts in the War.

The Khojas, " honourable gentlemen " as the name means, come in the main from Gujarát and Bombay. But they are scattered now through all the bigger trade centres of India—Calcutta, Nagpur, Sind and the Punjáb. They have not, however, confined their enterprise to the Indian Empire, but have made settlements in the East wherever the British flag gives its subjects protection. They have crossed the mountain passes to Hanza and Dardistan ; they have sailed to Zanzibar and the Persian Gulf ; they have penetrated into Arabia ; they maintain business connections with Singapore, China and Japan, and even with England, America and Australia. Many of the great commercial interests of India are in their hands, and in business they bear an excellent reputation for integrity and punctuality. Their representatives have an important place in the Legislative Councils of Bombay and of the Government of India. In social life, they are something of epicures, and their clubs are not only hospitable but are well-managed and furnished. The best of food and the best of wine will always be found at any entertainment given by these generous and liberal merchants. They enjoy literature and still more music and dancing ; and they are among the most tasteful supporters of those arts. Many among them have now forsaken commerce for the liberal professions.

The Khoja woman is hidden in seclusion behind the *purdah*. The few that are to be seen are as a rule somewhat below the middle height and are of a graceful, but not altogether healthy, slightness. They are well educated and are good housekeepers, known for their neatness and management. As Mussulmans they are of course married under a system of free contract, but unfortunately for them Hindu tradition has been too strong, and they suffer in practice from many of the disabilities of their Hindu sisters. Remarriage after widowhood is in practice almost unknown; and divorce is so discountenanced that its relief is seldom sought. On the other hand, the ascetic idea is at least absent, and a wife expects and a husband is prepared to give constant attention and all possible comfort. They have a force of character which merits this attention; and their features, with arched head and broad forehead, strong chin, and large lustrous eyes, are the index of their character.

Of other trading classes of Mussulmans, the Memans, also converts from Hindu castes in Sind, Kathiawád and Cutch, deserve notice, if only for their charity and piety. All Memans, women as well as men, hope to perform the pilgrimage to Mecca and habitually visit the Chisti Shrine at Ajmer. And for their large secret charities the women, no less than the men, have a well-deserved reputation.

Among the large body of middle-class Mussulmans of the usual Sunni sects, those who claim to be descended from foreign invaders and who are at least not directly traceable to any special wholesale conversion, the position of women is on the whole satisfactory and agreeable. Every family has its poor relations and dependants so that, even when she is childless, the mistress of the house is seldom lonely. The morning she spends at her toilet and in seeing to the day's marketings and looking to the kitchen. At meals all the family, men and women alike, meet and eat together. Sometimes, even, a much-favoured friend of the husband's, a trusted and intimate friend, may be introduced to the inner, unveiled circle. After the midday meal, a rest; then sewing and talking; then games of backgammon and chess make the afternoon pass. The evening dinner then needs looking to, and after dinner it is common to hear or read tales and romances or religious books. Children may also take up much of the woman's time; and among Mussulmans as a rule the wife may count upon a loving, almost a passionate, husband, except in the unhappy cases where differences of temperament produce a real antipathy. In that case she can always try to force a divorce from his hands, though the practice varies with the social circle. That the pressure of Indian influences has forced upon them child-marriage, followed only too often by premature consummation; that the intentions of the Prophet in regard to divorce and widowhood have often been neglected; and that the rule of veiling has been interpreted with a superstitious irrationalism, quite opposed to the teachings of the law, are disabilities under which the Mussulman

MEMAN LADY WALKING

woman of the middle classes still has in part to suffer. But she is at least oppressed by no tradition of renunciation or asceticism, and she has, in favour of her fulfilment and just cherishing, text after text in the sacred Book. The recent tendency to a purer Islamic practice, hand in hand with the growth of rationalism, offer her hope of early liberation from extraneous bonds and of development as a free human agent. The women of Islam have as guide rules of law, sanctioned by revelation, which if practised are more rational and more insistent on justice and human freedom than any other precepts ever codified into statutes. It is to be hoped that the recent advance and rationalistic movement in Islamic countries will secure the happiness that should follow intelligent practice of a humane code. The devastation caused by Mongol invasions and ravages and the subtle perversions induced by an alien atmosphere have to be repaired and eradicated; but there is no intrinsic reason why the social system of Islam should not again reach and surpass the high level it commanded in the days of Al Ma'mun.

In a review of the middle classes of India, it would be impossible to omit the rich and influential sect of Parsis. Descendants of the ancient inhabitants of Persia, expelled after the Mussulman conquest, followers of Zoroaster and worshippers of fire, they reached the west coast of India after many perils, to be finally protected by a Hindu Rána or prince. Small in numbers, for many centuries they lived in the main by agriculture, though there were a few among them who achieved a name in arms. With the coming of the British they changed their pursuits and their social habits. Commerce had heretofore been strictly protected by the exclusive guilds of the Hindu merchants. Its doors were now thrown open. Moreover, the British official required body-servants, if possible of good class. The Hindu was precluded from accepting such an occupation by caste rules of purity and caste prohibitions. The Zoroastrian religion left the Parsi free from such scruples. Many members of the community, by commerce direct and by the assistance that gratitude was ready to bestow, were soon able to insinuate themselves into positions which they maintained by their adaptability and their commercial integrity. In shipbuilding they excelled, and both in this and in the kindred trade of ship-broking they accumulated many fortunes. The liquor trade was their monopoly; and, aided by the privilege of exclusive distilling and a monopoly of sale, it was remunerative to an undreamt degree. By the end of the eighteenth century, an old traveller notes, practically the whole of Malabar Hill, the most fashionable and only really enjoyable portion of Bombay had already passed into the ownership of rich Parsis. Throughout the nineteenth century their wealth and their importance grew.

One of the most striking qualities of the Parsi community is its aptitude for imitation. With the advent of British rule, this facility stood them in good stead. It was not long before English education became general and almost universal among them, while by their prompt acquisition of the minor conventions of manners, they easily opened the doors of European society. In consequence it was not long before they attained a position of social importance, based upon solid grounds of wealth and education. The Parsi woman was not left behind in the advance of her caste. Many women studied diligently and even passed the examinations of the University. In general they demanded a liberty such as they read of in English novels, and fancied they could see among their English friends. They refused to marry except at their own choice. For the dull details of household management they expressed contempt and considered their duties done when they looked to the furnishing and decoration of their houses. In dress, the Parsi woman has contrived no less to modify her own costume, originally a slightly altered form of the Hindu woman's, in imitation of European fashion. She still retains the mantle or *sari*, but it is hemmed with a border imported from London or Paris. An outer lace shirt is draped like a blouse under the mantle. The trousers, which she has to wear under her skirt by customary prescription, are so curtailed as to be invisible, and the feet are thrust into silk stockings and Louis Quinze shoes. Her jewelry is of European pattern, usually second-rate, and she despises the beautiful antique designs of the Indian goldsmith as "old-fashioned."

The Parsi woman has in the past been greeted by an amount of praise from European writers which, though intelligible, is yet almost extravagant. It was natural to be pleased at so conscious an imitation, especially in a generation when most Europeans had no doubt of the superiority of their own civilization and were prone to judge the merits of other races, like missionaries, by their aptitude for assimilating its products. They could, after all, always clinch the argument by pointing irrefutably to the triumphs of the Albert Memorial and the Crystal Palace. In a country where few women of the better classes appear in public and beauty is seldom displayed, the spectacle of many gaily-dressed ladies, with graceful drapery, promenading along an Indian street with the freedom of a popular sea-side resort at home, gave almost as much pleasure and pride to the gratified Englishman as it did to the girls' own parents. It has required closer inspection and broader judgment of East and West to notice the cracks that stretch, no doubt inevitably, across the charming picture. New liberties, imitation not always too wisely conceived, above all sudden commercial prosperity—these have had their advantages. But they also have their countervailing losses.

At the bottom of such disadvantages as appear is no doubt the broad fact that the community as a whole consists of business men. There are of course individuals who have adopted the learned professions and are solicitors, doctors, barristers, and judges. But even they live in a society and probably in a family circle which is wholly commercial; and even their successes are estimated by the money they bring in. In many ways Parsi society is like the Jewish society that is to be found in the larger cities of Europe. But the Jews as a community are devoted to the arts and have a ripe sense of emotional and spiritual values. They respect learning and artistic expression. Even those—the greater number—among them who are engaged in business frankly enough recognize their inferiority to thinkers and artists. Again the Jews have always had a tradition of aristocracy among themselves, and in recent years have sought every opportunity of mingling with the nobilities of the countries to which they belong. The best among them have, therefore, raised themselves by art and letters and by an aristocratic code far above the narrow vices of a commercial middle class, and it is only the lower strata who continue to display the typical defects of " business life." But the Parsis have unfortunately so far missed these mitigations. They have not, and, within the memory of history, they have never had, the tradition of an aristocracy. They are separated from the indigenous nobility, not only by religion, but by interest and custom, and the difference has been deepened by their partiality for an Anglicized mode of life. Though a few among them have done good work, they have no real liking for learning and art. Hence there is hardly a community in the world, except perhaps in the United States of America, which bases its standards so largely upon wealth. Men are esteemed mainly by what they have managed to acquire; precedence is allowed according to size of income; the business man takes rank over the professional; and a memorandum of their richest men is inscribed on each Parsi's heart, as on tablets of brass.

These are defects which are not unnatural when a small and isolated community finds itself confined to commerce and is from its history devoid of higher interests. They are defects which do not alter the fact that not a few among the Parsis, especially those who have for generations reposed upon inherited wealth and have taken to the learned professions, are charming men and women and true and worthy friends. Among those who have such a position—who do not aspire to dazzle fashion in the wealthiest circles and do not require to increase their incomes by further trading—the women are attractive by their education and their rational freedom. They preserve a place of dignity and reserve, while quietly taking from life the benefits it offers to a liberal mind. They may even rise above the touchy vanity which is all too common.

It must, however, be admitted that Parsi womanhood has suffered harm from the excessive imitation of English habits—or what are taken to be such. From the nature of the case, because of their own inclinations and environment, the English life they have sought to imitate has inevitably been that of the middle classes. And the effect has been heightened by the enormous consumption of English novels among Parsi women. Owing partly to national character and partly to the demoralizing secret censorship which broods over the publishing world, nearly all English novels have to be "pretty-pretty" falsehoods, distorted away from the facts of life and the truths of nature. The consequence has been to produce a dangerous mental confusion in which spirituality and idealism are suppressed and replaced by a fruitless sentimentality. Reality on the other hand is known and presented only in the shape of hard cash. The harm done by such popular writings is not so apparent in England, where they are part of the normal tissue wastage of the nation. In a foreign and not immune constitution, they produce rapid inflammation. One finds therefore among Parsi women, as one does among the women of the United States, a mentality in which impracticable and silly sentimentalism is mixed up inextricably with a thirst for the solid advantages of wealth. They sigh for courtships of the kind depicted in their favourite "literature," with scores of "dears" and "darlings" scribbled over scented letters, with moon-calf glances and clammy squeezings of hands; they and the heroes of their fancy get photographed together like any German *braut* and *brautigam*; they enter marriage with a blind eye turned to the hard realities of human nature, to discipline for instance and duty, but with the expectation of finding a husband on his knees to pamper every wish and petulance. Yet at the same time, the Parsi, like the American, girl will not let herself slide into these sentimentalities till she is assured of her admirer's income and position. Both restraints—that which keeps her from love till she knows how money stands, and that which keeps her during her courtship within the bounds of technical chastity—come easy enough as she is, with a few honourable exceptions, free from passion. She would never give herself to the wild love of Romeo and Juliet or the abandoned ecstasy of Tristan and Isolde. Hermann and Dorothea, or a drawing-room ballad, would appeal more readily to her sympathies. That in England there is also another type of womanhood, truer and greater, she does not know—how could she? That there are girls of a fine candour and simplicity who are taught in childhood to obey and to have quiet, effacing manners, who respect a father whom they see controlling a large estate, honoured in Parliament, perhaps governing a great dependency, who are bred in a society of equals in which true and natural superiorities alone, whether of age or seniority, of success in the hunting-field or in the council, are admitted and publicly recognized, that such girls bring to their husbands with their love, respect, and the heritage of discipline, that as wives, while expecting to find fulfilment and the realization of their hopes, they are ready to subserve the higher and enduring interests of a family, of such facts and such nobilities of life—worthy indeed of imitation if such there must be—there can be little knowledge. Vital facts are not always plain upon the surface, and in England no class is so quiet and unobtrusive as the one which really counts.

The prevalence of a money standard in their lives has introduced among the Parsis the great evil of excessive dowries. Generally speaking, it may almost be said, no Parsi young man will marry a bride unless

PARSI FASHION

her parents come down with a large settlement, and scandalous stories are sometimes told of the means employed to extort larger sums from the father. The girl whose family is poor—be she as beautiful as Shirin and virtuous as an angel—stands in every danger of being left a spinster. Day by day the probabilities against marriage grow heavier, and the number of unmarried Parsi women of mature age goes on increasing. Alone of all the peoples of India among them the reproachful name of "old maid" can be used. The numbers of unmarried women are already so great that this has become a serious danger to the community, as for that matter it is among the upper middle classes of Great Britain. "Old maid-ism" must have its consequences: hysteria and other illness is on the increase; and the suffragette may soon become as actual a terror and a retribution to the Parsis as she has been in England. If this should ever happen, then climate and the surrounding environment are likely to make the pathology of the situation even more critical in India.

The marriage law which governs the Parsis is very much the same as that which exists in England. Marriages are strictly monogamous and divorce can be given only by the decree of a public Court of Law on grounds nearly the same as those admitted in the English Courts. In practice early marriage has ceased to exist, and indeed marriages, as in England, are as a rule contracted at far too late an age. The same causes which lead so often to women remaining unmarried, have also raised the average of age.

Parsi life presents, therefore, the picture of a society in which woman have many seeming and some actual advantages, but in which, on the other hand, they are more and more rapidly plunging into unforeseen but very real evils. They have great liberty, a liberty greater, or at least less restrained, than is enjoyed by the women of the better classes in England or in France. They can have education and the pleasures of a liberal mind. In accepting a husband they are ostensibly allowed full freedom of choice, though in practice they are of course limited by the usual considerations, by the importance attached to wealth, and, especially, by the great difficulty of securing any husband at all. They have the advantage of being trained to mix without shyness in all societies. But, even apart from a certain self-assertiveness which at times distresses their best admirers, they have to suffer from the growing probability of a life-long spinsterhood. Only too many will have to face the final misfortune of a wasted and infructuous life.

The community is distinguished by its loyalty and its generosity ; and Parsi women, as well as men, play their part in that lavish distribution of charity for which their race has become famous. It could be hoped that, without foregoing what they have gained in education and position, they should also preserve fresh the emotional values of sweet and disciplined womanhood and be able to secure those timely and assured conjugal relations which must be its fulfilment and best reward.

Working and Aboriginal Classes

"Sweetly the drum is beaten and
Sweetly the girl comes to draw water :
Sweet is the ochre on her forehead :
Sweet is her bodice of silk :
Sweet is her charming footstep.
Ohé ! the cakes baked by the girl :
Sweet is the girl with her infant child.
Lo, her dress is wet and clinging from the water
And she is adorned with tassels of jewels :
On her hands are bracelets
And her feet are enriched with anklets."

Rowing Song of the Fisher Kolis.

"A palmer came over the mountains and sat down under a barren tamarind tree
Then he got him three stones and placed a pot upon them.
He went to the midst of the town to ask alms and played his pipe as he went.
The sound of his pipe reached the ear of Rádha.
She ran towards her father and towards her mother :
'You are my father and my mother : I am going off with this palmer for my man.'
'Do not go, my dearest daughter, I will give you all you want.
Cows and buffaloes will I give and for your service four handmaidens.'
'What should I do with your cows and buffaloes ?
What should I do with your four maid-servants ?
For such a man have I prayed to God for full twelve years.' "

Marriage Song of the Fisher Kolis.

DYER GIRL IN AHMEDABAD

Chapter VI

THE WORKING AND ABORIGINAL CLASSES

If it was difficult in any way to summarize the varying conditions of the middle classes and to present with anything like unity some picture of their women, to attempt the same for the lower classes is to face difficulties that are in fact insuperable. The middle classes, as in all countries, are much conventionalized, and are always busied with a conscious effort to live up to an ideal that may be misapprehended or incomplete, but is still in the main intelligible. The differences that exist are either geographical or sectarian —differences due to tradition and development in differing environment, in varying faiths, for instance, and doctrines. The lower classes, especially the aboriginal tribes, still stand so narrowly on the circumference of the Hindu system that, with a literal eccentricity, they evade the attraction of conventional rule and regulation. They are governed by customs, often of immemorial antiquity, which may be outside the orbit of Hindu precept, and by superstitious fears which lead to sudden and capricious divagations. The main criterion of their status and the chief factor of divergence in their lives is the degree to which they have accepted Hindu Law or, to put it more exactly, the Brahman customs recorded in Sanscrit scriptures and stereotyped in the decisions of the Law Courts.

Broadly speaking, throughout India proper, the lower classes that stand within the Hindu system are the offspring of mixed Scythian and Dravidian parentage. But neither term can be taken too strictly. In Scythian may be included not only the hordes of White Huns, Gujjars, and Kusháns, but even some remote trace of earlier conquerors of Aryan race: Dravidian is little more than a collective name for the dark peoples who, before the dawn of history, were in possession of the Indian continent. From the two races in mixed and varying proportion are sprung the artisans and respectable cultivators of India, probably even the untouchable and degraded castes that cluster in dirty hovels on the outskirts of every village. In the far south they are almost, if not quite, Dravidian; in the north-west, where the five rivers flow, they are nearly pure Scythian. Between the two extremes are a multitude of shades and a multitude of customs. Even the Mussulman lower classes are in the main descended from the same constituents. Converts to Islam though they are and legally free to marry as they please among believers, they have usually restricted themselves to their fellows and have continued the line unbroken as it ran in the days of idolatry. The pretty dyer girl whose bright clothes and open smiling face is so much a feature of Ahmedabad, for instance, is by descent no different from her Hindu sisters. Where she has altered, where her gait

MUSSULMAN WEAVER

is more free and her glance more bold and frank, the change is due to that influence of belief upon physique, to which far too little attention has so far been paid by the professors of anthropology. This influence of mind upon body can be seen in Europe where the Jews, descendants of so many peoples and, at least as far as Eastern Europe is concerned, mainly Ugro-Turkish by race, have yet by an unanimous and constant habit of thought largely acquired the marked cast of features which is called "Semitic." In India the Mussulman population is a living instance of the same modification of the physical by the mental. The change has been too much ignored by a science which, from its mathematical prepossessions, thinks only in things that can be weighed or counted and neglects forces which must be measured by a subtler calculus.

The Mussulman weaver women, again, bear sons who are known for their turbulence and who strike home in every sectarian riot. Yet the Hindu weavers of the same kin are quiet and even timid. The handsome Sunni Bohora women of Broach and Cambay, converted descendants of the prevailing caste of Hindu cultivators in the province, are famous not only for their looks—and striking is their bold beauty—but also for their virile energy and resolution.

In the Hindu artisan and cultivating classes, the status of women is most affected by the social position accorded to the caste as a whole. The higher the importance of the caste and the more it acquires wealth and consideration, the more quickly it accepts child-marriage and—what is socially even more important—the prohibition of widow remarriage. These in India are the tests of fashion; and each caste, or even any single section of a caste, as it finds its position improving, confirms and establishes it by the fresh burden that it throws upon its womankind. For the enhanced consideration gained by wealth, and the ceremonial purity which can be bought by wealth, the women pay. Life-long widowhood is the price extorted from the individual for the social prestige of the class.

In the last thirty years a remarkable and quite the most important feature of Indian history has been the rapid growth and extension of Hinduism. Yet, so easy and natural has it been, it has passed almost unnoticed. There are many in Europe who believe that Indian castes are fixed, immanent, and immutable. And this belief is upheld with conviction by almost every Indian. Yet nothing could be more erroneous. The concept of caste is no doubt ancient and of a strength so confirmed that it can almost with propriety be called permanent. Yet the actual castes—the things that *are*—are fluid in the extreme and are in constant movement, while the boundaries of the system have recently had vast extensions. The ease of communication given by railways has brought the central Brahman influences home to every hamlet in the continent, till whole tribes that were formerly hostile have been persuaded to adopt the name and many of the customs of the Hindu. At the same time new thoughts of Indian nationality and solidarity,

CAMBAY TYPE

born of English education, have roused in the higher and educated classes a real desire to comprise within the Hindu fold peoples from whom their fathers would have shrunk as from foreign and debased savages. But the idea round which the whole caste system revolves is that of marriage. Far above the maintenance of ceremonial purity, far above mere restrictions on food and water, stands, as the one essential rule of caste, the limitation of lawful marriage to a fixed circle of descent, real or fanciful. And with this limitation, which is of the very essence of Hinduism, goes a certain view of marriage as magical, sacramental. Thus each additional conversion of a strange tribe to the Hindu system brings fresh adherents in great numbers to what, more or less clearly adumbrated, is at least a reflection of the Brahman ideal of womanhood. To coarser minds and to tribes not much advanced beyond the savage, only a thin ray of the ideal can penetrate. Among such tribes the woman may remain free for some long time from the trammels of the higher law.

For that law can be tolerable only when it is fully comprehended. But as they advance in civilization and the conversion to Hinduism is solidified, as it were, by developing education, so the ideal, more and more clearly grasped, begins to be followed in practice. It is at this stage that child-marriage and the unrelieved doom of widowhood are introduced. New India therefore presents the paradox that while in the upper class a few, gained to the cause of rationalism, allow widows to remarry, discarding almost with violence the old sanctions and the old beliefs, side by side in the great mass of the people the prejudice daily grows and millions now forbid remarriage who thirty years ago would never have dreamt of the restriction.

But as a whole the properly Hinduized lower castes have no great interest to the observer. The conduct of the women is as close as possible an imitation of the better class, deflected as in all countries by poverty and labour and by the inevitable roughness and coarser understanding of their class. To trace in detail the full recent growth and development of such a caste might have its interest, but would transgress the purpose and limits of this book. Of especial interest, should anyone attempt it, would be the development of the dairyman and milkmaid class in India. Divided into many septs, and in some instances differing now in race, they are descended from the Scythian tribes of Gujjar and Ahir. It would be interesting to trace them from the uplands of Kashmir, where they still roam, through the Gangetic plain to Káthiawád, where among many pretty women their women—Cháran and Rabári—are perhaps the most beautiful, and where their men are genealogists and bards, and stand surety for the treaty bonds of kings. Even in appearance, and greatly still in custom, they have much of the high mountain air of the great plateaux on the roof of Asia, where once they wandered with their sheep over dry, wind-swept uplands.

More homogenous and far more thoroughly imbued in the Hindu tint are the striking fisher or Són Koli caste of the western coasts. The collective name of

THE MILKMAID

Koli covers a multitude of tribes—not yet fully embraced in the Hindu caste system—whose unity of name and manifold distinction in fact forms one of the most difficult of the unexplained problems of Indian ethnology. A century ago most of their tribes were freebooters, cattle-lifters, caterans. Many Koli families won themselves little principalities, and some have got themselves recognized among the Rajput clans. Others are peaceful cultivators, and there are many who live as labourers by the sweat of their brow. But to this day there are some who prefer crime, and will even board a running train to rob the goods waggons. All of them have, perhaps, some strain of descent from an earlier race—Kolarian, or call it what you will—settled in India before the Aryan invasions. But it is clear that, though they retained a tribal organization, they must in great but varying proportion have mingled with and assumed the characters of other races. In places they are hard to distinguish from the aboriginal Bhil ; in other regions—in Káthiawád, for instance, and the salt plains where the receding sea has made way between Gujarát and Sind—they seem rather to be the residue of a Rajput soldiery, common soldiers perhaps, not ennobled by a diplomatic victory, or married to women of some earlier tribe. At any rate among some of these tribes there subsist traces of customs foreign to the rest of India, such as the rule of marrying an elder brother's widow or of the younger brother, even before her widowhood, sharing in her favours.

But of community with those wilder clans there is

now little trace in the customs of the fisher tribes who live upon the shore that stretches from north of Bombay City down towards the Malabar coast. In the past a certain fondness for piracy was perhaps a solitary sign of a probable connection. From their appearance, however, it is clear that they are the descendants of a people as widely distinguished on the one hand from the darker farming and labouring castes who form the major part of the population, as on the other they are from the grey-eyed and pallid Brahmans of the coast who are its spiritual aristocracy. Distinguished physically from the other inhabitants by their light-brown complexion, the round curves of their faces, and their smiling expressions, they are equally distinguished by their occupation, their separate dialect, and their aristocratic constitution. It is also clear that from the date of their settlement on the coast-line, they have kept themselves unusually unaffected either by the amours or by the moral and mental ideals of the surrounding population. History is not plain in the matter of their arrival on the coast, but a probable inference from tradition is that most of the present day Kolis are descended from immigrants who came down from the hills some four hundred years ago. It was only about two centuries ago, under the rule of the Peshwas, that they entered the fold of Hinduism, and they themselves say that they were first taught to know the Gods at that time by one Kálu Bhagat, an ascetic who had himself been of their tribe.

They are peaceful enough now, but they are still bold sailors, and it is their fishing-boats which bring the daily catch to the Bombay market. The men are handsome and well-built, with curious scarlet caps, like an ascetic's, which are the distinctive uniform of their class. But, as would seem in all countries to be the case with fisher-folk, where the man toils on the sea and on shore rests and smokes in idleness, in the daily round of life it is the woman who counts most. At home she is mistress, and she takes the earnings of her man and gives him what he needs for his drink and smoke. She carries the fish to market and drives her bargain with keen shrewdness. She does not lose as a saleswoman by the attraction of her smiling lips, showing her sound white teeth, and of her trim, tight figure. The dress is striking. The skimpy mantle or *sari* is slung tight between the legs and over the upper thigh, so that every movement of limb and curve of figure shows in bold lines, as the fisherwoman carries her basket on her head to the crowded market. The freedom and strength that they draw from the ocean is preserved by a customary law which allows women a reasonable liberty. In many ways the Koli fishwife is as fine and independent as her sister of Newhaven in Scotland. Like her, she has her share of her husband's drink when there are guests in the house or the sorrow of the swirling, driving rain is forgotten in a cheering glass. On their right hand these women wear a silvern bracelet of peculiar and heavy shape such as is worn by no other caste. No other bangle or bracelet, ornament or jewel is worn on that hand; and the absence of such adornments is for them a sign of the covenant under which God protects his fishers from the perils of the deep.

Among the fisher-folk marriages are seldom contracted till after puberty and the bridegroom is usually required to have attained at least twenty years. For they hold that a youngster below that age cannot work as he should at oar and sail, if he have a wife to cherish. The wife is usually consulted by her parents and asked whether she is willing to accept her suitor. Widows are of course allowed to marry again, and a full divorce is granted to a husband only if his wife be taken in adultery. In other cases, only orders of what can be called "judicial separation" are passed—with the same natural results that in England follow upon such decrees. Among the many castes of India, there is usually a constitution which can fairly be called democratic; disputes are decided and case-law made by an elected tribunal. The fisher-folk have other ways. The final decision in their caste rests with an hereditary headman aided, but not bound, by assessors. He gives decrees of divorce, in which the claims of the wife are treated with more justice than would be got from an elected and therefore hide-bound tribunal. In all cases of desertion, misuse, cruelty and neglect, whether accidental or intended, the wife can get a speedy separation by the order of the headman. On him again rests the duty of providing for all orphan girls and finding them good

A FISHWIFE OF BOMBAY

husbands. Further, the headman, sitting by himself "in chambers," has the right of protecting women who become mothers without being wives, of fining their paramours, and of finding them husbands to cover their disgrace. There are signs, unhappily, of the power passing—to be replaced by the usual elected body and rules derived more strictly from Brahman custom. But in the meantime women fare well, and their own bright faces, their healthy children, and their contented husbands all testify to the value of a practice as sane as it is unusual. Happiness readily expresses itself in song, and the songs of the fisher-folk are stirring and tuneful. They sing them in a dialect of their own, apart from the written language; and on their festivals it is inspiriting to hear the choruses of men and women joyfully chanting these songs of the sea.

Of aboriginal tribes pure and simple—creatures untamed and almost untouched by the various civilizations that one after another have shaped humanity in the Indian continent—there are many still left in the wilder forests and mountains. But the latest of the great civilizations that have reached India has set in action forces which they can no longer elude. A law that is at once impartial and all-embracing and a railroad system which, in search of trade, penetrates the jungle and tunnels through the rock, have brought even their homes within the economy of modern life. They are being quickly sucked into the vortex of Hinduism, to emerge half-stifled as a menial class. As at the touch they leave their strangeness and their jungle ways, they sink to the lowest scale among the civilized, where once, with all the dangers of wild animals and exposure to disease, they had at least been free of the forest. Among the smaller aboriginal tribes the Todas of the Nilghiri mountains are conspicuous. For one thing they are an instance which reduces to absurdity the inferences of an anthropology too subject to abstractions and too reliant on skull-measurement. For anthropologists of that school have found the measurements of the Todas to be exactly Aryan—the one thing which—(if the word is to have any meaning at all) they cannot be. The Todas are a small tribe now, some 700 persons in all. They support themselves by rearing buffaloes, whose milk and cheese they sell to the residents of the neighbouring sanatorium, recently built upon a mountain plateau that for hundreds of years had been thought impenetrable. In the spring they scatter with their herds through the pastures of the uplands and return to their dirty huts in the rainy season. But the touch of the finger of civilization has crushed their loins, and the decay of this curious tribe is too far advanced to be arrested. Drink, opium, and poverty have contributed to their ruin, and the tribe is scourged by the ravages of a disease to which they were new. The women are vicious without emotion, and mercenary without disgust. Miscarriages are frequent, and those children who see the light are born diseased, are left neglected, and die like flies.

Of all the aboriginal peoples—more important even than the Gond peoples and the Gond Rajas of Central

TODA WOMAN IN THE NILGIRIES

India—the greatest and the most impressive are the Bhil tribes. They can be traced from the first dawn of history; and in all the Sanscrit poems, Bhil queens hospitable to errant Aryan knights are as needful an incident as Bhil archers, liker devils than men, shooting their death-dealing arrows from behind rock and bush. They held kingdoms and had founded temples, reservoirs and towns when first they met the fair warriors from the north. Then they were driven forth and hunted and slain, and their homes were made desolate and they took to the forests as broken men, their hand against all others. Century after century they lay hidden in their lairs, coming forth only to rob and raid, cruel and merciless since they themselves were dealt with cruelly and without mercy. Yet one thing they were always, autochthonic, like some primeval force in whom, if all could have their rights, the soil and its title must to the end be vested. And so it is that to this day they have by a curious prescription a symbolic function at the coronation of Rajput princes. When a ruler first ascends his throne, by a Hindu custom, a mark of ochre is printed on his brow by a priest as an auspicious omen and a sign of fortune. But for the Rajput chiefs who rule in the country that was once the Bhils', the mark must be made by blood pricked from the finger or toe of a Bhil tribesman or his sister. Even the first and proudest chief in India, the Mahárána of Mewár, does thus acknowledge the autochthonous race whom he displaces but who hold the prior right.

From Mewár the Bhil tribes reach west to the confines of Gujarát and south to the Deccan plateau. Their status varies as the land they occupy is more or less open and cultivated. In the forests they are independent and self-sufficient, ruled by their own tribal custom, rough perhaps and uncultured, but merry, equal one to the other, not unprosperous. In the civilized tracts, where economic forces of competition have free-play and Hinduism has prevailed, they have sunk to the position of a proletariat, supporting themselves on labour such as they can get and by theft whenever possible. They lose their virtues at the contact and merge on the untouchable masses of the lowest Hindu castes, with the same vices and the same imitative rules and customs.

On the hills and in the forests of the Rewa Kántha States and Mewár, however, the Bhils are seen at their best—sporting, loyal, happy wildmen of the woods. They have no villages like the Hindu plainsmen—close-crowded and ill-smelling. Each family has its own homestead in the clearing, a hut of logs . grass-thatched, overgrown by the creeper-gourd with its yellow flowers. The men are skilled in the use of bow and arrow and love to roam the forests after game. They follow the tracks by which wild animals move at dawn from the valleys, and they know each lair or water-hole. The women also know the forest, where they collect grass seeds to be ground to flour, and where they gather the luscious fleshy flower of the mhowra tree to cook into cakes or distil into fiery

GOND WOMAN

liquor. They keep large numbers of cattle and every homestead has its own fowls and chickens. Two enemies only prey upon them, the leopard who seizes the grazing calf, and the anopheles mosquito which injects into their blood the malaria that ages and kills them early. For the rest while the years are good and the seasons kindly and the rain comes in good time and falls sufficiently, they are happy and free from care. But when there is scarcity, they die of famine, save for the relief brought to their doors by British administration.

Among the hill tribes, where they still distinguish themselves from the Hindus, the Bhil woman has much freedom. When she has long passed puberty, at seventeen say or eighteen, she marries pretty much as she pleases. They are, in a pale copy of the Rajput feudal chivalry, divided into clans and have the religious prohibition of marriage within the clan. The girl must, therefore, choose a husband from another family. But the clan descents are rather vague and blurred, and the prohibition does not in practice hamper their choice seriously. Outside of this limit, at any rate, they marry with their heart. Only the intending bridegroom must make the girl's father a customary payment of money or of cattle, often stolen in a raid from some lowland village. If he cannot pay, however, he has the option of doing seven years' service in the father's house, as Jacob did for Leah. During that time he is free of the girl, though he is not fully married till the end, and he lives in the house more as a dependent poor relation than a servant. Till they are married, the girls are not expected to be too strictly virtuous. While they are young, their sport with neighbours' boys is merely smiled at indulgently as "the play of children." Even when they have ripened to real womanhood—"and then Chloe first learnt that what had happened near the forest was but the play of shepherds"—they still wear the white bodice which shows them to be girls unclaimed by any man, and no one looks too closely to their actions. When once, however, they have chosen their husband and settled down to marriage, it is rare indeed that there be thought of any other man. Rare above all is it, if there have been children of the marriage. If, however, there should be trouble, divorce is easily arranged by a small payment to the husband and the wife is free to marry another man. A widow of course is no less free to marry, and a young woman never remains in widowhood. Men and women live on very equal terms, and there is much good-humoured affection between husband and wife and children. Not unlike is it to the life of the Scottish peasant and his wife, an easy freedom in youth leading to a homely and loving marriage. The money that they earn is often kept by the housewife, who allows her man so much per week for drink, the chief diversion of the Bhil. She also is none too strict and likes her glass at a festival. But the woman is usually temperate, while the man only too often drinks to a wild excess.

The Bhil women, deep-breasted, broad, their large thighs showing bare, look fit to be the mothers of

BHIL GIRL

sound children, healthy and strong. Pleasant and even comely they appear, with their flat, good-natured faces and their plump limbs, their features a little coarse perhaps, but sonsy. Their hair lies low on the brow in a pleated fringe, caught on the crown by a bell-shaped silver brooch. They are fond, like all savages, of adornment, and layer upon layer of glass beads, dark blue, white and crimson, lie heavy over neck and breast. Heavy bands of brass circle the leg from knee to instep, and clash and tinkle as they move. A coarse cloak of navy blue, draped from the head over the body, is tucked up into the waist-band, leaving the thighs half-bare. They look men boldly in the face, with candour and self-reliance.

The Bhils, both men and women, are fond of a joke, and nowhere in India is laughter heard more freely and more readily. The more Rabelaisian the joke, it must be allowed, the better they relish it; and women are as openly amused by an indecency as men. Their songs are not always lady-like, and a wedding song gives them full scope for merry ballads, of a sort common in Europe up to the seventeenth century but foreign to the drawing-rooms of to-day, which have room only for a Zola or an Ibsen. Laughter the Bhils have and loyalty, good-nature and simple hearts. What they have in their minds they speak openly; and plain words can surely be forgiven, when the thought is straight and true.

Dancing is one of the great amusements of the Bhils, both men and women, and they should be seen dancing at the spring Saturnalia, the festival of the Holi. They light a large bonfire of teak-wood logs, throwing into the flames handfuls of grain as an offering to the local goddess. Then the dance proceeds round the blazing fire. The men carry light sticks in their hands, which they tap against each other, at first slowly and listlessly, as they begin to circle slowly round. In the centre the drummers stand, beating the skins in wild harmony. Then the dance grows wilder and always wilder, and the dancers shout the shrill whoop, not unlike the Highlander's when he dances, a yell which quavers from the compressed throat through quickly trilling lips. As the time quickens, the sticks are beaten faster upon each other, and the dancers move three steps forward, then a turn, then three steps forward, once again. The women also dance round and round, and their shrill voices begin a song. The men follow the words and reply, verse to verse, in a weird antiphony. When the fun becomes louder, the men join hands in a circle and the women climb up by their clasped hands till on each man's shoulders there stands a woman, her hands also joined to her neighbour's, and the whole circle revolves to the tune of some village song. When they are not dancing, jests and jibe are bandied freely between the younger lads and their girls, and now and again a loving look or touch is rewarded with a ringing box on the ears.

But, with all their freedom, the Bhil women have their pride and virtue. From their womanhood and independence they will not readily derogate, even if the price be heavy. And not seldom the stranger, some stall-fed Hindu from a fatter land, has learnt this to his cost. There was such a one, a Charge Officer, who administered (or was supposed to) a relief camp in the Bhil country during a famine year. Being well-fed and lazy, pampered and a fool, he thought he could have his will of the bold, " unlady-like " forest women who were forced by famine to seek relief at his hands. So he cast a lecherous eye on one who was young and fair and had a merry laugh. And being fat and foolish, he put the alternative to her bluntly, as such a man would, with no nonsense about it. If she was not pleased, she could look out for herself elsewhere. So she smiled a merry smile and fixed an hour when he should meet her in the forest. But when he got there, he found not her alone whom he sought but with her a round dozen of her women friends. And each one had a good, fresh-cut stick in her hand. Then they explained to him at some length, and with free and appropriate gesture, that they knew exactly where to use a stick with most effect. Their language was distinctly daring, but they left him clear about their meaning. And that after all is the main thing. It took him quite a long time to get home after they had done with him, and crawling through the jungle is not pleasant going. Even when he was dismissed from his employment a couple of days later, the impression of their arguments was still acute. But there were hopes that in time he would begin to understand the character of the Bhil woman.

Such manners and such characters it would be difficult to find elsewhere in India. With the general Hindu ideal of service, chastity, and effacement they have no common ground. Yet it cannot be doubted that here is a life which makes for happiness and, in its own way, for self-realization. The Bhils are wild and uncultured, of course, and they have to suffer from the fevers of the forest and from wild animals. Of luxury they know nothing and their pleasures are primitive and rather coarse. But they are contented. The wife loves her man and the husband cherishes his wife with a very real fondness and even with respect, and they have a cheerful pride as they watch their children play and grow strong and upright. They share their hardships and their small joys fairly and equally. They tend their garden with a kindly contentment; and at night, their labour done, they drink their glass and have their jest, and go to bed in the forest clearing tired and comfortable. And when the Bhil does rob a travelling merchant and is caught, it is for his wife alone that he yearns in the dreary separation of the prison.

Civilization, if it comes to the Bhil from the East, brings with it child-marriage and Brahman law and caste degradation; if from the West, it brings the factory and the industrial slum. Drunken and thriftless, oppressed by customs which he cannot understand, he finds himself submerged in the lowest proletariat, exploited and despised. Can civilization give anything to the Bhil better than what he has ?—ease and liberty!

The Dancing Girl

"She measures every measure, everywhere
Meets art with art. Sometimes as if in doubt,
Not perfect yet and fearing to be out,
Trails her plain ditty in one long-spun note
Through the sleek passage of her open throat,
A clear unwrinkled song: then doth she point it
With tender accents, and severely joint it
By short diminutions."

Music's Duel. CRASHAW.

"Nowadays Indian 'reformers' in the name of 'civilization and science' seek to persuade the *muralis* (girls dedicated to the Gods) that they are 'plunged in a career of degradation.' No doubt in time the would-be moralists will drive the *muralis* out of their temples and their homes, deprive them of all self-respect, and convert them into wretched outcastes, all in the cause of 'civilization and science.' So it is that early reformers create for the reformers of a later day the task of humanizing life afresh."

Sex in Relation to Society. HAVELOCK ELLIS.

Chapter VII

THE DANCING GIRL

For the women of India an independent profession is a thing almost unknown. Here are no busy typewriters, no female clerks, no barmaids. The woman spends her whole life in a home, supported and maintained, her father's as a child, then her husband's, or else one of those large joint households in which every woman of the family, widowed or married, finds her place. If she is poor, she may have work to do in plenty, besides the care of her house and children. She may sew or go out to help in richer households; often she joins her husband in his work, and you may see the potter's wife fetching earth and carrying bricks, or the washerman's wife drive his laden ox. Sometimes she labours in the field, busily weeding or bent double as in the water-covered muddy patch she transplants the young rice-shoots. But in none of these tasks does she work for herself, alone and independent, at a trade chosen by her own taste. She labours as one member of a higher unit, the family of which she is a part, and she knows that by her efforts she helps to feed and clothe her children or to add to the funds controlled by the head of the joint family. Even domestic service, in the European sense of the word, hardly exists. Ruling and noble families have their maid-servants, but these are not independent women hired under a contract, enforceable at law. They are women born and bred in the palace, bound by affection and upbringing, hereditary house-servants, almost slaves. They are treated as of the family, are paid by food and clothing, by presents and the final gift in marriage to a male servant. Only a few, a very few there are, widows mainly, usually Mussulman, who can in the Western sense of the word be called servants.

In recent years changes in ideas, and still more changes in social economy, have produced a few women in regard to whose work it is possible to use the words "independent profession." There are even a few lady doctors, Parsis mainly, in whose case the imitation of European customs and the resultant obstacles to marriage have facilitated study and the adoption of a career. There are far more who are teachers—always underpaid—in girls' schools, or nurses—also underpaid—or midwives. Largely these are Brahman widows, who, repudiating the austerities of traditional belief, have found a more useful life by these labours, and relieve their relatives of the charge of their support or bring up their children by their own praiseworthy efforts.

But even these are still exceptions to be counted by hundreds, by thousands at the most, out of all the three hundred millions of India's population. For the women of India, it may almost be said, there is only one independent profession open, one that is immemorial, remunerative, even honoured, and that is the profession of the dancing girl. There is hardly a town in India, however small, which has not its group of dancing girls, dubious perhaps and mediocre ; and there is not a wedding, hardly an entertainment of any circumstance, at which the dancing girl's services are not engaged. And it may be added that there is hardly a class so much misjudged or a profession so much misunderstood.

For long generations and in many countries the dancing girls of India have been the theme of poets and stock figures of romanticism. In Indian literature it was of course natural that they should find a place. And in fact, from the earliest Sanscrit poets down to the novelists and play-wrights of modern Bengal or Gujarát, there are few dramas in which a dancer does not play a rôle. Often the part is pathetic, even tragic, while it is usually edifying and pietistic. The courtesan who, urged by the eloquence or attraction of a pious ascetic, finds the grace of God and abandons art for austerity and the palace for the hermitage, is one of the recurrent conventions of the Indian classics. In one of the best-known of Mahrathi poems, there is such a picture, expressed with vigour and emotion. Converted to self-denial and renunciation, the dancing girl, once beautiful, lies alone, dirty and squalid, without food, in a witch-haunted graveyard, affrighted by ghosts, tormented by spirits of evil, yet uplifted by the love of God and blessed by her memories of the saint whose coldness was to her the sign of a higher adoration. But in the literature of Europe the bayadère, to use a name corrupted from the Portuguese, has also been a frequent and a luxurious figure. In the romantic fancies of the late eighteenth and the early nineteenth centuries, she was, both in France and Germany, a personage on whom poets lavished the embellishments of their art. Her hazy outlines they bespangled with the imagery of fiction and the phantasies of invention. She was a symbol for oriental opulence, a creature of incredible luxury and uncurbed sensuousness, or tropic passion and jewelled magnificence. From her tresses blew the perfumes of lust; on her lips, like honey sweet, distilled the poisons of vice; hidden in her bodice of gold brocade she carried the dagger with which she killed.

Divest her of poetic association. Rob her of the hues cast by the distant dreams of romanticism. Strip her even of the facts of history and the traditions of the Indian classics. Yet she remains a figure sufficiently remarkable. Not tragic and certainly not gay, she embodies in herself so much of India, both its past and present, that without understanding her life and significance it is impossible to comprehend the social whole which she explains and commentates.

The very name of dancing girl, it must be noted, is a misnomer. For as an artist she finds expression primarily in song, not in the dance. In the Indian theory of music, dancing is but an adjunct, one rhythm the more, to the sung melody. It is the singer's voice

DANCER IN MIRZAPUR

which is the ultimate means of music, her song which is its real purpose. To embellish its expression and heighten its enjoyment the singer takes the aid of instruments, the pipe, the strings, the drum and not least of the dance. Regarded in its first elements, the dance is one means the more of marking the time of the melody. Throughout the Indian dance the feet, like the tuned drums, are means to mark the beats. The time is divided into syllables or bars and the dancer's beating feet, circled with a belt of jingling bells, must move and pause in the strictest accordance. The right foot performs the major part, the left completes the rhythmic syllable. But further by her dance the singer's art is to make more clear and more magnetic the meaning of her song. With her attitudes and gestures she accords her person to her melody and sense, till her whole being, voice and movement, is but one living emotion. Her veil half-drawn over her features, her head averted, a frown wrinkling her brow, she portrays modesty recoiling from a lover. With joined hands uplifted to her forehead, with body bent, and eyes cast upon the ground, she accompanies the hymns of worship and resignation to God's will. With quickly moving gesture, she marks the harsher sounds of rage or mortified indignation. Even pleasure and the tenderer joy she represents by the softly swaying body and slow waving movements of her upturned hands. But it is not enough that gesture should be natural and appropriate. Mere realism would not harmonize with the songs and instrumental music to which it is an accompaniment. Its crudities would be out of tune, conspicuous, even brutal. The dancer's gestures and pantomime must be soft, rhythmic, and restrained. Like every other art, dancing too has its economy and its self-restraint. And the way to this ideal harmony is through the simplifications of convention and the discipline of a graceful technique. The dancer has to learn by painful practice to move her limbs in harmony with the rhythms of her melody, to avoid all that is abrupt or unsymmetrical. Each pose should be that of a statue, emotion poising in a harmony of line and balance. In order to attain this complete accord of movement and melody, this union of grace and emotional expression, it is necessary to conventionalize the means by strict attention to the material presented to the creative artist—in the case of the dance, the youthful female figure. As in a painting, to the trained eye, a line presents the transition between two differently lit surfaces, so in the dance, by an habitual agreement between the spectator and the performer, certain simple movements are made to evoke wider imaginations. Indian dancing, like every art, must have its own conventions. But they are conventions finally based upon actual mimicry, simplifications, one may say, of natural movements. They are attained by the exclusion of all that is superfluous, leaving only the essential curve or contour of the movement. They are the actual made spiritual, by the excision of all excess, by the suppression of the uncouthness which defective material and stiff muscles force upon human action. The movements of the Indian dancer bear to the primitive gestures of men and women, in the moments of actual impulse, the same relation as the simplified form of Indian painting and sculpture bear to the realities of living flesh and blood in light and shadow. To the European the conventions are difficult to understand, as they presuppose a different training ; and in him they do not readily awake the required emotion. For European art has for many centuries been in the main realistic, concerned above all with the material appearance of things and actions. The art of the East, on the other hand, has in all its leading schools sought the spiritual, striving with the jejunest outlines to interpret the significance which may underlie the outward clothing of form and colour and surface. Moreover, the oriental eye has a natural aptitude for decorative pattern, to which the excessive devotion of the Indian intellect to deduction and abstract analysis affords a parallel. The artist, therefore, does not rest content with simplification but further seeks to manipulate the conventions, through which he realizes his spiritual meaning, into a symmetric and decorative pattern. The same tendencies appear in the dance, when practised as an art, in India.

There are two great methods of artistic dancing in India which correspond to the main geographical distinction of the continent and can be called the Peninsular and the Northern. The Peninsular or Southern has its home and training-ground in Madras, where the temple dancing girls, the "servants of God" as they are called in the vernacular, follow their fine tradition. The old Hindu city of Tanjore with its exuberant temple is the centre of the school, to which it has given its name. The other or Northern method is at its highest in the cities of Delhi and Lucknow, more secular in its purpose, yet more austere in its expression.

In the North where the girls, wearing an adaptation of the Mussulman dress, are mostly of that faith and have no bond with any temple or religious institution, the dance or gesture-play is strictly subordinate to the song. The artist moves back and forward a few steps as she sings, the feet of course always beating the time, while her hands are raised or lowered and her fingers grouped in a few conventional poses, gracefully artificial or simply decorative, but with no present actuality and little stimulus to emotion. The pleasure of the spectator is in the main intellectual, the effect of reminiscence and association, while he interprets the meaning of which the movements are suggestive but abstract symbols. At the end of the verse the dancer floats softly round the circle of spectators, with coquetry in her eyes, extorting applause by a quick virtuosity of steps and pirouettes, which have little relation to any living and real passion.

The Peninsular school, on the other hand, gives the dance in and by itself a far higher value and more extended field. It is far more than the mere visible decoration of a sung melody. It has a life of its own, often wild and passionate; and has its own instant appeal to independent emotions. Often the dance is in itself the pantomime of a whole story, the meeting and love of Krishna and Rádha, for instance, at the river's side. The melody of the instruments is a suitable accompaniment and the voice does little more than supply a pleasing refrain. Sometimes it is a mere rhythmic and decorative reconstruction of everyday actions, the mimicry, harmonious and graceful, of a boy flying a kite or of a fluttering butterfly. The dancers move lightly and quickly over the floor, their steps diversified, their gestures free and natural. Upon their features play the lines of hope and joy, of sorrow and disdain. Then as the story closes, in a final burst of melody, their voices rise with the instruments that accompany in a last *forte* repetition of the refrain or motive.

Thus in the Peninsular or Tanjore school the art of dancing, though also, of course, dependent upon conventionalisms of gesture and movement, and significant of meanings which it suggests rather than imitates, has a more actual appeal to emotion and a less fettered freedom. It has a finer spontaneity, a freer flow of imagination. At its best, it is a splendid school of dancing, the only method perhaps worthy to be put beside, though below, the magnificent creations of the Russian ballet.

From the point of view of art, however, even the Tanjore dancing girls, and still more the performers of the Northern school, have certain defects, which could be removable if the players and public had a finer sense of artistic purpose. The women themselves are too often of little education, illiterate, with their tastes uncultivated. A good voice and some natural grace, with training only in technique, may make a pleasing enough dancer but cannot produce an artist. For any excellent attainment a higher cultivation is required. Another difficulty, peculiar to India, is that many experts will, from superstitious fear or jealousy, refuse to impart their secrets to a pupil or a novice. But worst of all by far is that lack of artistic sensibility, general in modern India, which is satisfied by the tricks of virtuosity and has no recognition of sincerity and deeper beauty. In song the faults are obvious and regretted. High notes are screamed out with the utmost effort of the singers' lungs to the amazement and admiration of the groundlings, while the practice of slurred arpeggios at the highest speed obscures the roundness of the voice in the true melody. Given a good voice, a girl is only too soon trained to these efforts, on which in a few years her natural gifts are squandered. Smooth and easy singing and finished phrasing are little valued by the side of those difficult but unbeautiful accomplishments. Similarly in the accompanying dance violent gestures, strained poses, or undue and difficult effort ravish praise that should more correctly be given to sincere emotion and an easy and natural rhythm. A dead conventionalism, emphasized and over-strained by difficult contortions, has repressed

MUSSULMAN NAUTCH-GIRL

the development of the art, especially in the northern, more abstract method.

Another great drawback against which Indian professional dancing struggles is the lack of a public that itself is given to dancing. For every art the great safeguard and vivifying influence is a popular practice of its easier forms. Music flourished in Italy and in Germany, where every person sings. Poetry becomes great when behind it there is a living growth of popular ballads or lyrics. The Russian ballet has made its wonderful achievement because every peasant dances with vigour and even with grace, and in the summer nights in every village young men and women dance. In India popular dancing has for many centuries been moribund, even dead. At the festival of the new Hindu year, in a few parts of India, groups of ladies sing songs in unison as they circle to a slow measure or rhythmic step. Occasionally in the *zanânas* of the richer families the ladies dance what is known as a Rásada. Each catches her neighbours' hands and they move round and round in a circle bowing, slow in the beginning and faster to the end. These are the palace dances, now almost disused, of which can be read in Sir Edwin Arnold's translation of the Chaurapanchasika :—

> "Yet now, this but abides, to picture smoothly
> How in the palace-dance foremost she paced:
> Her glancing feet and light limbs swayed demurely
> Moon-like, amid their cloudy robes ; moon-faced,
> With hips majestic under slender waist,
> And hair with gold and blooms braided and laced."

In villages among the lower classes there is also at stated seasons some rustic dancing, even with men, of a rough and boisterous kind. But generally speaking, popular dancing there is none. "No one dances unless he is drunk," the Indian gentlemen might mutter with the too grave Roman.

Still, granting these deficiencies of environment and allowing for all imperfections and desired improvements, dancing remains the most living and developed of existing Indian arts. In the Peninsular school above all, India has a possession of very real merit, on which no appreciation or encouragement can be thrown away. It is something of which the country can well be proud, almost the only thing left, perhaps, in the general death-like slumber of all imaginative work, which still has a true emotional response and value. It sends its call to a people's soul; it is alive and forceful.

All the more tragic is it, a very tragedy of irony, that the dance—the one really Indian art that remains—has been, by some curious perversion of reasoning, made the special object of attack by an advanced and reforming section of Indian publicists. They have chosen to do so on the score of morality—not that they allege the songs and dances to be immoral, if such these could be, but that they say the dancers are. Of the dances themselves no such allegation could, even by the wildest imagination, possibly be made. The songs are pure beside the ordinary verses of a comic opera, not to mention a music-hall in the capital of European civilization, Paris. The dancing is graceful and decorous, carefully draped and restrained. But the dancers, it is true, do not as a rule preserve that strict code of chastity which is exacted from the marrying woman. How the stringency or laxity of observance of this code by a performer can possibly affect the emotional and even national value of her art and performance has not been and cannot be explained. Art cannot be smirched by the sins of its followers; the flaws in the crystal goblet do not hurt the flavour of the wine.

In the Peninsula of India dancing and professional singing is first of all a religious institution, bound up with the worship of the Gods. To every temple of importance are attached bands of six, eight, or more girls, paid in free gifts of land or in money for the duties which they perform. They are recruited in infancy from various castes and wear the ordinary garments, slightly more ornamental, of the Indian lady of those regions. In certain castes the profession is hereditary, mother bringing up daughter in turn to these family accomplishments. In other cases, as in the great temple of Jejuri in the Deccan, children are dedicated by their parents to the service of God and left when they reach a riper age to the teaching and superintendence of the priests. Twice a day, morning and evening, they sing and dance within the temple to the greater glory of God; and at all the great public ceremonies and festivals they play their part in the solemnities. Teaching is imparted by older men, themselves singers, who take in hand the training of small groups of girls. In some cases a form of marriage is performed, for the fulfilment of traditional religious obligation, with a man of the dancer's caste, with an idol, or even with a sacred tree. But the ceremony entails no ethical obligations, such as apply to the real married woman. The dancers are regarded, being independent and self-supporting, as freed from the code which applies to women living in family homes and maintained by the work and earnings of a father or a husband. It is their right to live their lives as they will, for their own pleasure and happiness, unrestrained by any code more stringent than that of an independent man.

Besides Tanjore, the old Portuguese possession of Goa and the neighbouring districts bordering on the ocean, where the forests and rocks of the Western Ghauts drop sharply to the rice-lands of the shore, are famous for the excellence of their singers. Here they are known under the name of Naikins or "Ladyships," and have a position of no little respect. Though they like to trace their origin in their own sayings to those nymphs who in heaven are said to entertain the Gods, the truth is that they are largely recruited from other classes, whose children they purchase or adopt. They live in houses like those of the better-class Hindus, with broad verandahs and large court-yards, in which grows a plant or two of the sacred sweet basil. Their homes are furnished in the plain style of the Hindu householder, with mats and stools and wooden benches

DANCER FROM TANJORE

and an abundance of copper and brass pots and pans and water vessels. Only they wear a profusion of gold ornaments on head and wrists and fingers, a silver waist-band, and silver rings on their toes, and they make their hair gay with flowers. Their lives are simple and not luxurious; but the days are idled away in the languorous ease of the tropic sea breezes, a land of repose, a lazy land. They rise late, they bathe, they eat rice-gruel, and talk and sleep. The long afternoon is passed in more chatting and in their constant enjoyment of chewing betel leaves, till after dinner they go out to sing and dance to a late hour of the night. It is a life of quiet ease, uneventful, indolent no doubt, but hardly dissipated. And of course in all worship and religious observance they are devout and orthodox, fearing the Gods, and reverent to the officiating priesthood.

Now when some Hindu reformers object to the employment of such women in the temples of God and deny the efficacy of song and dance as adjuncts of religious emotion, it would of course be impertinence for the follower of another creed to express an opinion. The rubrics of prayer are between the worshipper alone and his God. If they preach that worship and oblation are for those only who have made asceticism their practice and who have turned their faces from the world to the pure concept of divinity, they are obviously within their rights: and the question must be decided by a congregation of fellow-worshippers. Even if they desire to bar the temple-door to women, who have taken no vow of chastity and hope for salvation without closing their ears to love, they are entitled to do as they like with their own, if they can obtain a consensus of believers. Observers of other creeds would willingly, if without impropriety they could have a voice, join in deploring the abuse, in some temples, of the custom of dedication; for girls thus dedicated, as at Jejuri, are often too numerous for the purposes of the temple-service and are thrown upon the world, without adequate artistic training, almost, one might say, with none, to make their way as best they can. When this happens, though Hindu society treats the devotees kindly and gives them easy admission to good houses, yet their dearth of artistic accomplishment, the refusal of support by the temple to which they are ascribed, and the pressing needs of sustenance must often force the unfortunate girl to a distasteful trade. But to include these among dancing girls in the proper sense is hardly fair. The motives of dedication are different and are exclusively religious, while the custom has arisen from the old Hindu tradition of appointing a girl to take the place of a son. The trained singer who succeeds to an appointment in a temple is in a very different position, and her life is as a rule happy and prosperous. The example of other countries has shown how an art may gain by the support of a Church, and how, in the absence of countervailing circumstances of popular understanding and enthusiasm, the withdrawal of ecclesiastical patronage may cause its decline and even its ruin. The Reformation in Europe, for instance, whatever its benefits to a new growing world in other matters, swept without doubt like a devastation over the rich fields of human imagination and like a tempest obliterated the æsthetic emotions in which the human soul attains its highest. In India, in the absence of a humanism such as Europe could imbibe from Athens, the dependence of art upon religion is more strait and isolated, while the very forms of Indian art are moulded in a supernatural conception of the universe. So subtly poised is it upon this pinnacle, that the mere touch of the freethinker and reformer, one fears, may send it shattered to the ground.

In the North, it has been said, the dancing girls have no connection with religious institutions, though, as it happens, their artistic conventions are more abstract and less sensuous. Mostly they are Mussulmans by belief or are Hindus who have adopted Mussulman ways and manners. They do not belong to colleges or groups but live alone and independently, earning their living by their art, without support from any temple. At the same time it is the custom in many parts to invite them to perform at the shrine of some dead saint during the annual celebrations. They sing on such occasions songs of a sacred kind, psalmodies of praise to God and His Prophet, poems well known in the Urdu language. They chant also the odes of the Sufis or Persian mystic poets, in which the adoration of the Deity is clothed in the language of love, and the praises of wine are metaphors for the ecstasies of the Spirit. Usually the dancing girl lives alone in her own house, some balconied and flat-roofed house in the crowded bazaar, where she can overlook the movement of the town and mark the doings of her world. There is little that escapes her prying eyes, and the musicians in her pay, the barber who lives in the street and the seller of betel leaves keep her posted in all the city scandals. There is constant coming and going to her doors, and in the afternoon admirers from the younger nobility and professional men drop in to pass the time and smoke and laugh a few hours away. Sometimes her house becomes a centre of intrigue where palace revolutions or doubtful conspiracies are hatched under her friendly eye by young men, who lounge on her cushions beside the trellised window. The room is heavy with the sweet, over-perfumed smoke of the black tobacco paste which she smokes in her silver-mounted hookah. When she drives out at evening, police-constables salute her. In most Native States such dancing girls, two or three or four, are an appanage of the royal retinue, and are paid salaries or retaining fees on a generous basis. Such a girl will ordinarily get one hundred to one hundred and fifty rupees per month from the State—the salary of a Police Magistrate—with gifts on special occasions. In exchange she has to sing twice or thrice a week when the chief calls for her, but with his permission she may always perform at other houses where she can earn larger fees. Some chiefs are famous for their taste, and a girl tries to secure an engagement for a year or two in such a Darbar to establish her reputation for the future. In many cases these dancers, as they grow older, marry one of their lovers and settle down to the quiet life of the respectable Mussulman lady behind the *purdah*. Sometimes they adopt a clever and pretty girl and train her, half as maid and half as companion, in the mysteries of their art, till she in turn becomes a singer and helps to keep her mistress and teacher, with no little piety and charity, in her old age.

Modern opponents of dancing, however, with their influence on a population which has few artistic tastes and a marked bent for economy, have already done much to degrade the profession and are gradually forcing girls, who would formerly have earned a decent competence with independence and an artist's pride, into a shameful traffic from very want. Day by day the number of those women is growing less who alone preserve the memory of a fine Indian art. And, as they lose the independence earned by a profession, day by day more women are being thrust into the abysmal shame and destitution of degraded womanhood. An Indian proverb already sums up this peculiar item of the "reform programme" thus: "The dancing girl was formerly fed with good food in the temple; now she turns somersaults for a beggar's rice."

But, for the delineation of Indian life and society, the position of the dancing girl must be envisaged from a loftier altitude. It is only from such an aspect that her portrait can be said to complete and interpret the gallery of Indian womanhood.

Indian Women

In the long history of human development occasional licence appears as necessary to mankind as the habitual routine of morality. Convention and self-restraint have been accepted and adopted for mutual convenience; but, by an impulse as natural as it is healthy, man has from time to time escaped from his stagnation through the orgy. Even the savage, with his underfed body and atrophied sensibilities, finds a periodic outlet for the starveling powers and ambitions hidden in his breast by some spring or autumn festival at which, by one wild orgy, he overleaps the fears and trammels of magical prescription and intoxicates himself, for a brief space, into a freer manhood. When savagery ends and barbarism begins, the orgy becomes something of an institution, as it did in the Christian Church of the Middle Ages or in the Holi of India. But as civilization grows more refined, it is for the spirit rather than the body that the outburst into freedom is demanded. In a cultured community it is a sort of cerebral licence which is excited and assuaged by the orgies of the imagination. The theatre and music, painting and poetry by their stimulation purge the soul of those emotions which, unrelieved, would sour and make ill the spirit. In a state where man is bound hand and foot to a mechanical routine of wage-earning, he must seek through the excitement of his imagination that explosion of emotion followed by quiescence, by which the fermenting activities of his mind and body can alone find their needed relief. Among the agents that rouse this excitement and in turn satisfy it are to be ranked high the rhythm and music of the dance, with the spectacle of graceful limbs and pretty faces, of dresses such as are seen in dreams and jewelry rich beyond phantasy. Every man at some time in his life has woven his fairy tales of hope, and there is none so dull but has pictured a goddess to his fancy. Now the woman who toils in his house and shares his interests may be ever so tenderly loved and cared for, but she is his own help-mate, of his own sturdy flesh and blood. Hardly—except perhaps for a space in the first blossoming of new love—can he clothe her familiar being with the robes and colours of his dreaming fancies. But in the trained actress with her artful graces and her aloofness, he sees one who responds to those secret aspirations, and gives them room to expand and calms and soothes them, till at last, the spectacle ended, and his mind reposed, he returns to his home in peace for the further routine of workaday existence.

Now where life is free and unrestricted, among the powerful and the leisured, every hour has its variety and desire may be satisfied without awaiting any special occasion. But when existence is narrowed to routine and one day is like another, then indeed the soul must sometimes soar to an illusion of wild wind-driven liberty. Man has to guide his plough in the furrow; but not to look to the sky and its currents at the turning!—better death at once than such weariness. And it is the finer creative spirits, the men that think and produce, who are quickest crushed by the unbroken rule of abstinence. In India the general tone is brown, the light grey-brown of dusty plains and dry fields and villages of sun-baked mud. The ritual of to-day is that of yesterday, and will be that of to-morrow. The same prayers, the same labours, the same plain food, the same simple house and furnishings. Simplicity, abstinence, repression, the rejection of all that is superfluous, these are the notes of ordinary life. There is contentment enough as a rule. The wife is faithful and devoted, the children play and grow up and get married, the cattle pull the plough and the soil bears the corn. It produces on the whole a contented resignation, this life, with its austere simplicities and its overhanging haze of asceticism. But even then there are times when the self will out and the lulled nerves begin to stir and tingle and stab with a bitter pain. There is no social life as in France and upper-class England, where ladies of wit and reading, graceful, well-dressed, trained to charm and please, quicken the minds and respond to the sympathies of a wider circle, while at the same time imposing a fine code of manners and a tactful moderation. The wife, devoted and affectionate as she is, must usually be first the *house*-wife, busied with a narrow routine, limited in experience, bounded by babies and the day's dinner. In most classes she is illiterate and she has few of the accomplishments which amuse and distract. Even in Athens, the city above all of urbanity, as the married woman was secluded and domestic like the Indian, the female

NAIKIN IN KAṆAṚA

comrade, the *hetaira*, with her witty talk and her song and accomplishments was a necessity of social life. In old India also this need was known, as can be read in the traditional poetic histories, and the dancing girl, the *gunika* as they called her, was the recognized teacher to young princes of manners and of chivalry. Those days are past; but even now the dancing girls, by the admission even of a missionary,[1] "are the most accomplished women among the Hindus. They read, write, sing and play as well as dance." They dress well and modestly, they know the arts of pleasing, and their success is in the main due to the contrast by which they transcend the ordinary woman and to the illusions they can give. They do not, therefore, merely fulfil a need but also represent an ideal. Even apart from their art and its high imaginative value, as almost the only living art in India, they respond in a larger sense to a real need of society. To stifle a class of women, living their own lives in independence, graceful, accomplished, often clever, to degrade them, to make them outcastes and force them into shameful by-ways, is not merely to sin against charity; it is also a blunder against life.

The existence of such a class, regarded in the light of ultimate truths, may fall far short of the perfect state. But the remedy in any country lies not in their repression and degradation, the most disastrous of all attempts. It lies in the freedom and education of the married woman. When the married woman also is

[1] The Rev. M. Phillips, "Evolution of Hinduism," 1903.

freed from the oppression of narrow codes and the dull monotony of housework, when she too is able to be accomplished and graceful, witty and artistic, free to choose as she pleases and to be true to her nature, then no doubt the professional beauty must by the mere weight of facts become extinct. But what nation, what society will risk the experiment ? and what conditions can make it possible ? This at least is clear that where a rigid matrimonial system, supported by all the sanctions of religion and inspired by a tradition of asceticism, is fast entrenched and fortified, where woman is limited and narrowed to the duties of a housekeeper or a mother, there the fulfilment of the deeper cravings of human emotion and the satisfaction of artistic sensibilities will depend upon a class that has in it much which is not ignoble.

Woman's Dress

"Upon my right hand did stand the Queen in a vesture of gold wrought about in divers colours."

Psalm XLV.

GIPSY WOMAN

Chapter VIII

WOMAN'S DRESS

Dress in India can be comprised within a few typical forms. Fashion, which in Europe is so frequently variable and occupies itself with line and contour, is in India far more stable and persistent. Fashion exists, of course, as in every land where women live and grow and change. But it busies itself rather with what may be called the accidents than with the essentials of attire. In the choice of colour the women of India display a rich variety ; and selection, though less subject to sudden and violent alteration, is governed by those moods of temperament which are generalized under the name of fashion. No less operative is changing temperament upon the designs of jewelry and the choice of gems to set in gold. Even in respect of the textures which women choose for their clothes, there are collective changes of mood and mode to be noticed. But in point of dress and adornment, as in most other activities, in India there is a governance by authority and a quasi-religious sanction which is foreign to the strongly individualist tempers of the West. The shapes and to some extent even the colour of dress and the design and manner of wearing jewelry are among those distinctive marks of social rank and ceremonial purity, in a word of caste, which are guarded jealously as if almost sacrosanct. It is only in the additions and embellishments permitted upon the normal habits of the caste that the human personality finds room for self-display. A woman must first of all make her dress conform to the approved habits of her class. That done, she is free to express her own tastes and talents within the range of such permissible colours and superfluous ornaments as do not alter the essential lines of her costume.

The interest of dress centres mainly upon the human psychology of which it is one among many other expressions. And it is not a little surprising that this inner and living bond has so often escaped the writers who have made costume their subject. Dress, regarded as form and colour only, has no doubt its own value to the painter. Like every arrangement in which selected hues or lines are grouped for the creation of a new beauty, it has an emotional appeal apart from its meaning or history. The uses of drapery in sculpture and the sensuous pleasure given by rich velvets and gold brocades in the paintings of Titian or Veronese are instances of the fascination of clothes, merely on their decorative side. But an intenser interest comes to being when dress is known to be also the expression of a character that in one sense may be called individual but may with more reality be regarded as part of a vast national life.

For by its very nature dress is a means selected to heighten the attraction of the sexes for each other.

Woman's Dress

The use of clothes as a protection against the extremes of climate is merely secondary and is even something of a reproach to natural adaptation. It is as adornment, and in its purpose of attraction, that it has its real and ultimate meaning. That dress comes to be used incidentally to preserve modesty does not affect its primary purpose. Modesty itself is one of the secondary properties of love and one of its most powerful weapons. But it is when mankind becomes sophisticated that the value and function of modesty are properly understood; and it is then that dress and ornament are so designed as to combine their direct and, under the guise of modesty, their indirect attractions. It follows, therefore, that in any people the use of the means of attraction which are supplied by dress and jewelry must correspond to the attributes of the persons whom it is desired to attract. If the dress did not conform to some inbred desire in those who see it, it could have no power to please; even it might become repellent. But similarity of birth and training tends to mould the majority of each nation to something of an average, and it is after all as a response to the desires of the average person that dress is designed. It responds, therefore, to the psychology of the people in which it is found.

Looked at from this aspect, the fundamental difference between the costumes of European and of Indian women becomes at once more deeply significant. In Europe, during the long centuries that have succeeded the fall of Rome, one quality above all has clung to dress, that is, *bizarrerie* of form. The Teutonic barbarians who uprooted the Mediterranean civilizations and imposed in their place those tribal feudalisms and customary rules from which Europe is not yet fully freed, seem whether from their primitive particularism or their inborn brutality to have largely been lacking in the sense of form. Symmetry and simplicity were conceptions beyond their northern brains and outside their temperament. Even to this day the German (who with least admixture of blood or education represents the primeval Teutonic savage) is hardly able by any effort of reason to comprehend the meaning of these words. In essence, it would seem, his mind is formless, vague, amorphous. So in their buildings, the Goths could find no use for purity of form. What they sought always and with a great effectiveness achieved was a shape, or rather a conglomeration of shapes, complicated and exaggerated, with lengthy spires and cumbrous altitudes, that should be curious, awful, and *bizarre*. They never sought to soothe the mind. Their churches do not so much attract attention, but capture it, as it were, by an audacious ravishment. And as this purpose was congenial to their own psychology, so did they win their effect among their own and kindred peoples. Similarly their women, if they were to excite the desires of men habituated to bloodshed and the strong stress of war, had to take their attention by storm, with the aid of the fantastic and unexpected in their costume. Without the subtlety of imagination and finesse to

A GURKHA'S WIFE

excel by a fine harmony or a graceful nicety, they were forced upon the extravagant and exuberant. The lines of their dress were not designed to be congruous with the human body or to agree in beautiful drapery, but were meant rather to amaze the onlooker by a sudden onslaught upon his vision. At any cost they were to be effective—to produce, that is, an immediate effect by the strangeness and extravagance of their form. In regard to colour they had less invention and hardly any taste; and the grey skies of the north are not suited to the richer hues. So it was to contortions of line and form that they had recourse. However mitigated, these are characteristics that remain to this day. Even in modern dress, the lines tend to be abrupt and exaggerated, and an ever-changing fashion varies them in a discordant manner. Every ten years, it has been said, the shape of womankind, as it is visible, changes in Europe. Each new change means, of course, an attempt to capture attention by a novel attitude. This is the cause that, out of the whole nineteenth century, it was only for a few years under the Consulate and early Empire that woman's dress appears tolerable to an artist's eye or even, upon reflection, to the common man or woman.

Indian dress, on the other hand, has this in common with the classic style, that it is simple in form and harmonious. It exacts no distortions or deformities. It veils the body but it does not misrepresent it. Still less does it attempt to substitute a fictitious for a natural line. But while the Indian mind, like that of the classic Mediterranean peoples, approves a natural simplicity of design, unlike the other, it delights in a profusion of extraneous ornament. Even the monstrous temples of the South are in essence simply planned, but they are overlaid and even overloaded with masses of strange carving and decoration. Indian psychology, in this not dissimilar from the Teuton, has a craving for the wonderful and *bizarre.* The people are of those that look for miracles. But, by a fortunate dispensation, they are content to leave the pure lines of form undisturbed—a quality that keeps them in regard to the broad facts of life true to nature. For their wayward fancies they find scope in *bizarrerie* of colour and external decoration. Thus the Indian woman wears dresses that in shape are easy and simple and beautiful, but she seeks further to attract by a marvellous variety of colour and a curious adornment.

The limits of the *bizarre* as it appears in India are probably reached in the dress of the *Banjara* women. They belong to a tribe that, far from unmixed, has in it much of that gipsy race, which has also migrated across the Sind deserts and Asia Minor to the furthest corners of Europe. For centuries they were the carriers of India, transporting salt and opium and grain on their pack-cattle along the trade-routes across the continent. They have settled down now, some of them, in little settlements where, under their own chieftains, they till the soil and deal in cows and buffaloes. But many of them are wanderers to this

A GLIMPSE AT A DOOR IN GUJARÁT

day, daring smugglers, dangerous when they are cornered, often even thieves and robbers. The men are especially handsome, with a free and fiery look, and a manly air. But the women also are not by any means unattractive, and the striking dress they have chosen, with its bold colours and its swinging skirt, sets them up well and handsomely. The pity is that they will wear it till from age and dirt it drops off with its own corruption. The bright colours they affect reach their limit in the pleated skirt with its glaring reds and yellows, a motley that has in it something of the clown or mountebank. The bodice in no real sense fulfils its part but is rather a bright-decked screen dropping from the neck to just below the waist-line, stiffened with pieces of glass and thick stitching. The mantle which they adopt, unlike that of most Hindu women, is short, like that of the Mussulman, but coarser. Their jewelry is peculiar to themselves, and in shape strange and striking. It is worn about the head in great profusion, so that the twinkling cunning face seems almost set in silver. The hair has two pleats at each side into which tassel-like ornaments of silver are hung. But most *bizarre* of all is the horn or stick, twined into their hair, which rests upon the head and props up their mantle like a tent. Originally perhaps designed to give the head a better protection against the eastern sun, it has now acquired a religious significance and is never doffed, even at night in bed, except by a widow. That with this inconvenient attachment, they still can balance by its nice adjustment heavy pots of water on their heads is one of the minor wonders of the Indian country-side. The Banjara encampment with its boldly-clad and boldly-staring women, also it may be added with its strong fierce dogs of special breed, is a sight too picturesque ever to be forgotten, especially in a country where life tends in the villages to a brown monotone.

The *bizarre* is again to be found prevailing even over form on the Mongolian borderland of Northern India. In Nepal, whence come the brave Gurkha soldiers of our wars, dress, like the shape and decoration of the wooden temples of the people, has in it something alien to the normal lines of Aryan and Indian womanhood. And the strangeness is heightened by the quaintness of the jewelry and the uncut turquoises in which they delight.

But in most of India proper the essence of dress is simple. Shoes are not in general worn, though loose wide slippers of velvet or of leather may be sometimes seen. The natural result is that the foot retains a beauty which can never be expected when it is cramped by constant pressure. The working woman, tramping miles along the roads or over fields, with heavy burdens on her head or her child upon the hip, loses of course too quickly the springing instep and sinks to a flat and sprawling foot. But in the higher classes, or among the womanhood whom caste preserves in a moderate seclusion, the foot is small, well-curved, and light. It is a thing of infinite fascination, tinted perhaps with the henna's pink, almost like a flower. Even aged women there are to be seen, their faces worn and wrinkled, who still have the unspoilt feet of youth and well-born blood. Among the richer ladies of the greater cities, where it is smart to be "advanced," Parisian shoes and silken stockings are nowadays worn, at least out of doors—a habit enforced by the security thus gained against plague infection; but the greater number still preserves the foot free and beautiful.

For the rest, among Hindu women the dress consists of three portions only, never more, though they may be only two. These are a skirt, a bodice, and a mantle. The skirt is not very different from the petticoat of Europe in cut, but may either drop simply or be made up in accordion pleats, something as a kilt is pleated, so cut as to stand out a considerable way at the ankle. The latter shape, worn mainly by the women of Márwár, but in painting invariably given to Rádha and the loves of the god Krishna, is most beautiful with its brush and swing. The skirt is fastened plainly by a silken cord tied fast at the waist and is sometimes girdled by a silver belt. The Indian bodice again is designed in the main to support the breast whose form it defines and even, by its pattern, accentuates. It may either fit all round the person, fastening in front by buttons or a ribbon, or be a covering for the chest only, put on from the front and tied across the open back by two tapes. But the most distinctive feature of all is certainly the glorious drapery of the *sari*, which has been translated "mantle" in default of a better word. The *sari* is an article of dress as distinctive as the Spanish mantilla and as difficult to wear with the right charm and manner. It is an oblong of material, hemmed when possible at one side with gold embroidery and edged with a sort of closed fringe. When, as is most common, it is worn with a skirt, its length is about fifteen feet and its breadth about three. When, however, as in a contrasting style, it has by its intricacies to take the place of an absent skirt as well, it measures some twenty-five feet in length. It is to these mantles that the Indian lady devotes her deftest thoughts and on them, within the limits conceded by caste and fashion, that she displays her personal tastes. Their hues and patterns have an infinite range. Some are in plain natural colours, white or red or blue—solid, unbroken colour, not least beautiful in the stark sunlight. Others are delicate cotton prints, flowered and sprigged and dainty. Sometimes they are printed in a bold decorative pattern, formal and conventional. Neutral and half tints at times mix in a bewildering wealth of hue, till the eye is at a loss to know whether the ground be green or pink or purple. The border may be a plain hem-stitch or a two-inch broad piece of gold brocade, sumptuously woven in the acanthus pattern or in the shape of birds and flowers. But in the draping of the mantle, so simple in cut yet of such infinite variety, consists the highest art and the true expression of personality. One end is taken round the waist a couple of times and tucked into the waistband

A WIDOW IN THE DECCAN

at the centre, falling to the feet in formal folds; the other passes over head and shoulder, with the breadth decorated and displayed across the upper half of the body. In the management of the upper half lies the true secret. It must show the full beauty of the cloth, yet by a sort of innocent accident, without a hint of ostentation. At the same time it must be loose enough to allow graceful folds to drop naturally from the head to the shoulders, and tight enough to sit close at the breast whose curves it accentuates while it seems to veil. Enough but not too much of the bodice must be shown with a fine nicety. The border is at times allowed to turn carelessly up, till the gold armlet above the elbow can be seen even on the covered right arm. At one moment, a modest gesture brings the mantle across the face, as in shy courtesy before an elder or an illustrious man; in a crowd it is draped to hide both arms and conceal the figure; when it slips, it is quickly drawn forward over the head with a charming pretence of timidity. The Márwári woman by a trick peculiar to herself makes of her mantle a screen held open between two fingers, through which only her lustrous eye appears, melting and languorous; and in the armoury of every Indian woman the mantle by its nice management is the chief instrument of love.

The short mantle, worn as described, should of course imply a skirt. But in the south of Gujarát, from Surat to Bombay, whether from the steamy warmth of the climate or from some subtle change of mood, ladies of the richer classes, while continuing to drape the mantle in the same graceful way, have of late years given up the usage of a skirt and wear at most a trim lace petticoat. The effect is not unlike that of a recent ephemeral fashion in Western Europe. Seen in the bold Indian sunlight, the double thicknesses of light silk or cotton are little less transparent than a veil of gauze and limbs are revealed in a shadowed fulness, which is less modest than it is suggestive.

In the Central plateau, however, and the south of India the skirt is also dispensed with by a fashion that can claim at once antiquity and respectability. There it is the long mantle, twenty-five feet in length, which is worn. Of thick coarse silk and dark solid colour, it is so draped as to be caught between the legs in a broad, low-hanging fold, tucked loosely at the back. Its folds are carefully arranged to leave a double thickness, marked by the border of the mantle, over the upper part of the legs. It is a style inherited from a remote antiquity, descendant from the dresses seen even on Buddhist carvings in the great rock temples of the Deccan. Beautiful it can hardly be called, with its effect of a divided skirt and its too clumsy folds and thicknesses; but it is certainly not frivolous. Rather perhaps should one say that it is eminently respectable, with its sameness and stiff conventionality. The pressure of the ascetic ideal is shown even more strongly in the monotonous colours, dark blue usually or dark green, which are the ordinary wear in those parts of the country. To the artist the

A WOMAN OF THE UNITED PROVINCES

costume, one would think, had little value; yet that it can be idealized is seen from the effects achieved in the simplifications of early sculpture. This contrast in dress between the southern part of the Peninsula and Gujarát or Northern India reflects once again that contrast in belief and character which has already, perhaps with a too frequent repetition, been remarked. This monotony of asceticism is even more noticeable in the south in the dress of widows (poor creatures with shaven heads, their limbs untouched by a single jewel!)—a dress of a mantle only, white or of a strange dull, dingy red—a dress that kills all looks and attractions, save where the light of religious duty, nature overcome, makes the starved face seem spiritual.

In the dress of Mussulman women the main feature is that trousers are substituted for the Hindu skirt. They may be wide and baggy, cut in loose full curves from the hips to the tighter openings at the ankles, a style not too precise to be devoid of all attraction. Or, as worn by ladies of the Upper Indian aristocracy and by other women who lay claim to Moghul descent, they may sit tight like gloves from ankle to knee, a fashion at once ugly and repellent. It would be difficult, even after long reflection, to design a style of dress so unbecoming to a woman's gait and figure, so crudely frank, so hideously unsuggestive. A bodice may or may not be worn, as Hindu influence is more or less strong. A long fine shirt, half open at the neck and falling to about the knee, is an invariable article of dress, which on a young woman fits well and gracefully. In former days, and even now among the older-fashioned, a long full-pleated skirt and jacket in one was worn above the other garments, fitting tight to below the breast, then from the high-set waistline spreading out in wide stiff pleats like a broad petticoat. Over her head the Mussulman lady wears a shawl or mantilla, less long than her Hindu sister's mantle, which is made of the finest textures and is dyed in the most delicate of colours. It is the full dress of the Mussulman lady that, except in Southern India, the dancing girl has made her own for professional uses and embellished with every device of pattern and every richness of material.

It would be interesting to digress here, in relation to Indian dress, upon that long conflict between the *decolleté* and the *retroussé*, which in Europe has from time to time been settled by the successes of the former. But a full discussion would go beyond the purpose and necessary limits of this book. Briefly it may be said that, in this matter too, Indian dress quite correctly expresses the difference which subsists between the present European and immemorial Indian temperament. For, with reasonable exceptions, it may be said that in India, on the whole, no special feelings, either of modesty or the reverse, attach to the lower limbs. The skirt is, therefore, not the hampering, stiff garment that it usually is in Europe. But the upper half of the body, on the other hand, has a far greater significance than in Western Europe. And this it is which has made the use of the covering mantle or *sari* the most distinctive feature of Indian costume.

Dress even in its simplest form has been seen to have its sectarian meaning and restrictions. A widow for instance, at least among orthodox Brahmans in the Peninsula, is limited to certain solid colours, never black or dark blue, red as a rule, or white. And every woman is restricted to definite shapes and cut. To transgress beyond these limits would be to offend against caste rules with a sanctity defended and sanctioned by a caste tribunal. But greater significance attaches to the use of jewelry. Some stones are valued for this or that magical virtue; certain metals can or must be used only at definite times and places: some shapes of ornament are bidden or forbidden to a certain caste. The prohibition against wearing gold upon the feet is the most obvious instance. Here a value of a magical kind, as a purifying agent, is ascribed to the metal, and its use was not allowed on limbs where it might be contaminated by the dust and dirt of the road. Only in royal families is the prescription ever disregarded; and even then only by few.

Of forms and modes of ornament peculiar to one caste and partly at least sanctified by superstition, something has already been said in describing the fisher and the gipsy women. But instances might be multiplied without end. Each section nearly of the community has at least one peculiar jewel, associated with a religious festival or a caste ceremony or belief.

Perhaps the most obvious examples are the charms and talismans freely worn by all classes of Mussulman women. In these the stones and their settings are the symbolic expressions of deep and mysterious thoughts and the instruments of a magical significance. On amulets of white jade or carnelian are inscribed in Arabic characters the highest names of the Most High. On other cartouches are engraved the sacred symbols of the Jewish Cabbalists, just as Hindus draw and venerate that sign of the Swastika which from the time of the Bronze Age has presented the beneficent motions of the sun. They have little boxes of chased gold in which are enclosed written charms to protect the wearer from the malice of jinns and the malevolence of the evil eye. On heart-shaped plates of silver they cut the sacred hand which persists in the escutcheon of Ulster baronets, and on others are inscribed the name of "Tileth" and the injunction, "Adam and Eve away from here."

But the use of jewelry has a religious tinge no less among Hindus. It is for instance a common belief that at least a speck of gold must be worn upon the person to ensure ceremonial purity. Thus in Northern India there are castes where married women wear plates of gold on some of the front teeth; while it is general when preparing the dead for the burning to attach a gold coin or ring to the corpse. Moreover, the wearing of jewelry by women is prescribed by the sacred text which says: "A wife being gaily adorned, her whole house is embellished, but if she be destitute of ornaments, all will be deprived of decoration." This again is one reason why there is so little change in the design. Variety there is, and indeed the number of ornaments, each with a different name and use, is almost bewildering. But in each kind the design passes from one to another generation almost unchanged, and the craftsman has no need to devise new forms and varying settings. What has been worn by the grandmother will be equally pleasing to the grand-daughter. When there is change and variety, it is only in the large commercial cities, where European patterns are being exploited to the ruin of indigenous craftsmanship.

The bracelet is the most significant and the nose-ring the most peculiar of Indian ornaments. For bracelets are above all the visible sign of marriage. Young girls before their wedding may wear bangles of many kinds: but the first act of widowhood is to discard them all. Some which are made of lac are peculiar to the married woman, and next to them in significance are the bangles of variegated glass which are so much appreciated. On the husband's death these are at once shattered; and the same breaking of bangles is the accompaniment of divorce. The nose-ring, as it is called in English, is only seldom in shape a ring. In Northern India indeed, in certain castes, a real ring of large diameter passes through the cartilage; and its effect is not beautiful. But in most places and classes, it is not so much a ring as a small cluster of gems affixed by one means or another to the nostril. That worn most commonly in the Deccan—a sort of brooch with a large almost triangular setting—is also clumsy and unbeautiful. Another type, worn by the cultivators of Gujarát, is like a button in which the jewelled top screws, through a hole bored in the nostril, into the lower half—a form no less ungainly. But Mussulmans adopt a different and more graceful form. Through the central cartilage of the nose a small gold wire passes on which drops a jewel, at its best a fine pear-shaped pearl, dangling down to the central curve of the upper lip. But the prettiest of all—a real aid this to a pretty face—is a small stud of a single diamond or ruby fixed almost at the corner of the left nostril. Here it has the value of a tiny beauty-spot, more attractive by its sheen, and draws the eye to the curve of a finely-chiselled nose and down to the petulant smiling lips.

Among the most beautiful of Indian ornaments are the *champlevé* enamels made by Sikh workers who have found a home in the pink city of Jaipur. In golden plaques they scrape little depressions which they fill with oxides of various metals, fixed by the nicely-varied temperature of fire. Gems also are worn in great profusion by the richer classes, though little by those who have to regard their ornaments also as an investment. To the poor of course the purchase of silver or gold jewelry is still the only form of saving with which they are familiar and in which they have confidence; and it is quite impossible even to guess the millions of bullion hoarded unproductively in this form in India. In regard to gems, many a superstitious belief still remains. Thus it is believed that in an evil conjunction of the sun the ruby is propitious, while the diamond is remedial against the baleful influences of the moon. On the day of the week named after Mars or War, the coral should be trusted, and the zircon is efficacious against Mercury known as Buddha. The pearl is specially designed for wear when Jupiter is dangerous. The cat's eye deflects the radiances of Venus and in the ascending node the emerald is sovereign. This lore of gems is set out at length in the *Ruby-garland* of Maharaja Surendra Mohan Tagore.

The graceful dress and finely-designed jewelry of the Indian women is a covering and an embellishment, suitable and, as a rule, singularly attractive. But the person that is so covered receives no less care. An almost scrupulous personal cleanliness is observed by nearly every woman. Among the gipsy and criminal tribes indeed clothes are worn until they drop off from age; and the untouchable castes who perform the lowest menial services and cluster in sordid hovels outside the village also leave much to be desired. In the crowded slums of the industrial cities, too, it is to be feared, there are many, especially of the professional beggars, who from vice or dulled apathy allow themselves to become foul and loathsome. But even the worst of these could perhaps be equalled in the mean streets of Europe. These degraded classes once out of account, however, there is no question that the niceties of personal cleanliness are followed in all ranks with a fine devotion which can be equalled only in the upper class of Europe. In some points they may put even those to shame though they cannot vie with the modern luxury of the English or French lady's bath, with its sponges and gloves and powders and perfumed salts. Washing in India is a religious ordinance, scrupulously observed, and the body is cleansed with water and made smooth like bronze with orpiment and tinged with henna and perfumed with the essence of flowers, till it is a mirror of purity, worthy of adornment and respect.

The Moving Finger

"A creed is a rod
And a crown is of night,
But this thing is God
To be man with thy might,
To grow straight in the strength of thy spirit and live out thy life
as the light.

. . . .

I bid you but *be*.
I have need not of prayer;
I have need of you free
As your mouths of mine air,
That my heart may be greater within me, beholding the fruits of
me fair."

Hertha. SWINBURNE.

Chapter IX

THE MOVING FINGER

The aim of this book has been as far as possible to show the Indian woman as she is, living and acting and expanding. But life, properly speaking, cannot be represented. Representation must always be of something that is already past and therefore lifeless and mechanical. It breaks off and pins down, like a specimen in a museum, a mere fragment out of the moving continuity of life. So a photograph for instance, when it impresses a discontinuous moment on the plate, merely fixes something which is artificial and unreal. Perhaps in literature it would be impossible to give vitality to the picture of an Indian woman, unless in the form of poetry or prose fiction. But the picture would then be endowed with personal character and an individual shape. Here it was desired rather to analyse national characteristics and to display the varieties of Indian womanhood and their values. It was necessary, therefore, to embody the typical rather than the personal and to lose something of concrete reality in the effort to generalize usual habits of mind and body. It is, however, true that neither man nor woman can ever be so well known, as through the ideals which they feel. In those ideals, in the spirit with which they meet the incidents of life, consists all that is most real and permanent in their actions. Other desires and emotions, peculiar to the individual, which help to make his whole concrete life, are after all unharmonized and, as it were, accidental. Essential are the thoughts which guide his purposes and the social atmosphere in which he breathes. Regarded in this way, the womanhood of India appears on the whole to be moving in all its million lives towards a more or less similar ideal, more or less clearly recognized as the social class rises or sinks in education and self-consciousness. There are, of course, exceptions. The nobility of Southern India form a social back-water, fed by other traditions from a secluded source. There are wild tribes on whose crude minds the common thought has hardly yet had time to become operative. And the Mussulman population is, at least in name, ruled by an ethic far more rationalistic and liberal. Yet there is not a class which in some form or other, however indirectly, has not had to submit to the supremacy of an ideal which in its purer lines is truly national. With the increased ease of communication and the rigidity given to accepted Brahman custom by the Courts of Law and common education, the movement towards the same ideal throughout the various communities has become more marked and rapid. Peculiarities of caste and race tend to be swamped in the general current. In a few cases, new diversities have come into existence, where, for instance, some of a small highly-educated class have revolted against traditional restrictions or sought a new salvation in the close imitation of European customs without a European environment. It is in the comprehension of these ideals, manifested in typical castes and classes, and of the social atmosphere that any real image of Indian womanhood can alone be formed.

But it is not enough to see a woman in her girlhood and growth, in her love and marriage, and in her relations to her family and society. To grasp her as she really is she should be seen also as a mother. For if love is a duty of womanhood, biologically the function of motherhood is even more important. It is the most decisive of all her functions in a primitive society. As the race advances, it does not lose its place, but beside it ascend other functions, first and most essential that of love or wifehood, and afterwards that of polishing and refining a mixed society. In value to each life and each generation, the greatest of these is certainly love; and the successful wife or mistress ranks higher in art and literature and with the finer spirits and civilizations than even the best of mothers. For the former implies gifts which are not only rarer but also emanate from higher and nobler qualities of mind, while it responds to needs which are felt above all by loftier natures. Maternity, on the other hand, is the instinct of reproduction in action, controlled by intelligent care and affection. It is not peculiar to the human being but is as strong a force in the animal. It is of course essential, like everything else that is primeval in our life; for humanity is broad-based upon the animal. But wifehood is a conception of the creative human intellect, a specialized object of human feelings. The perfect beloved is an ideal form created by a developed intellect and fastidious emotions.

Hence the worth of a nation's womanhood can best be estimated by the completeness with which they fulfil the inspirations of love and its devotion. And judged by this standard, the higher types in India need fear no comparison. Whenever race and belief have combined to resist the mere negatives of ascetic teaching, there is a rich literature of love, there is a mastery of rapture, and with it the constant service of undying devotion.

Yet fully to estimate the value of her life, it would be necessary also to watch the Indian woman in her performance of a mother's functions. The strength of her desire for children, the warmth and selflessness of her affection, the extent of her care and teaching, her readiness or unwillingness herself to learn the needs of childhood, above all, the place in her heart that she affords her children—all these are factors which should be not merely weighed or analyzed but actually felt by a creature intuition. But only another woman could have such comprehension or attain such intuition. No man—even in regard to the women of his own country, where he is illuminated by the examples of his mother and his wife—could have the needed sympathy, the necessary similarity of feeling, to comprehend the woman's emotions to the child she bears and over whose growth she watches. It would be impossible to attempt the task in a foreign country of women by whose side one has not grown from infancy.

Some points, however, which lend themselves to any observation, may be noted, all the more since they have not infrequently led to misunderstanding. It is the case undoubtedly that every Indian woman, whatever her rank or race, has a clamorous wish to bear children, above all a son, for her husband's sake. " How many children have you ? " is the first question every woman asks another. In order to get children they go on pilgrimages and tolerate austerities, they give alms to beggars and are deluded by impostors. A childless woman becomes only too readily the butt of scorn and even of her own self-reproach. Not to have borne a son is to the Indian woman to have missed her vocation and have failed in life. She has a certainty of belief—" She knows " she would say—that it is her function, even hers, to have children ; and if she be fruitful, she counts herself blessed. From these data, it has often been inferred that Indian women in all classes have an overpowering desire for motherhood and are especially mastered by the maternal instinct. But that this inference is wholly just, may well be doubted.

In the upper classes at least it must be admitted that the woman wishes for children because of reasoned and intelligible motives, and that these motives are so strong as to overcome any instinctive passions. And a will moved by a mere calculation of reason may be as powerful as and even more effective than an act of will which really responds to a deep and eternal, unreasoned, self-creating emotion. The Indian woman at any rate has every reason to desire to be a mother, above all the mother of a son. Hindu science and philosophy have never hidden from her that, regarded as a living being merely like any other animal, her primary function is to continue the race. And religion has impressed this teaching upon every mind by the legend that a man's soul can be released from the torments which follow death only by the prayers and ritual of a living son. Moreover, she fears that barrenness may impose the presence of a second wife, a rival in that love to which, after all, she gives first place. Then, again, the end may prove to be subjection to another woman's son, heir to his mother's hatreds. Or at the best there is the pressure of religious faith—to think herself accursed, if she has no child, while even her husband may in time shrink from her as from a being judged by the doom of God. All these are motives which can be weighed by the intellect but which move desire and will-power. Yet their action does not in itself show that the instinct of maternity is strong beyond the usual.

It is true of course that little girls in India in their games are accustomed to play at being mothers and cook for imaginary children and put their dolls to bed, and in a word play as girls do all over the world. But so they play also at being wives and greeting their husbands and bowing to a mother-in-law. When it is considered how early they learn the secrets of life and how few their other games and amusements can be, it is hardly astonishing that motherhood should enter soon in their thoughts and pastimes. But the European child is at least as ready to play with dolls and as fond of mothering her pets with a mimicry to which her instincts call her. Where the European girl differs is that marriage enters little into her thoughts and games, love in any real sense hardly at all; whereas the Indian girl from childhood has her mind filled with glad anticipations, and responds to the name of marriage with a ready and not altogether unconscious emotion. Even from the example of the child, then, the inference would rather be that the instinct for love is quickly developed than that the maternal instinct is stronger than in other peoples.

There are considerations of many kinds which go to show that the desire for love is first in the Indian woman's heart, at least in the higher and better nurtured classes. In England for instance it is really now the case—largely owing to the defects of a highly artificial education and partly from the evils produced by bad economic conditions—that there are quite a number of women who would desire to be mothers but who actually look upon marriage and love as a distasteful and unpleasant preliminary. Such a perversion of view, it can at once be said, is unknown in India—not only unknown indeed, but even inconceivable. Every woman may wish for a child, but she wishes first and above all for the blessing of a loving husband, and she desires the child mainly to satisfy and conciliate the man to whom she gives herself joyfully.

Again it is striking that the whole long record of Indian literature contains hardly one picture of a mother's love, and is dumb even about the longing at her heart for a child. Erotic poetry is full and voluminous and the love of man and woman is sung in burning words in thousands of lyrics, while it is also depicted with a more objective grandeur in numerous epics. Hardly any European literature, at least since Alexandria, can vie with this literature of love in volume and intensity. But in the poetry of the West, mother's love has had its honoured place. In the letters of India it is almost absent.

It is sometimes suggested in India, and it may perhaps be true, that in the castes which allow divorce, a mother's affection for her child is a passion stronger than her love for her husband. It would indeed sometimes seem in those classes that she would more readily choose to sacrifice the father than the child. But it does not follow that the cause lies in the freedom of divorce, even though it be a factor which co-operates in the result. For in practice the Hindu castes which allow divorce are almost all of the lower class—in some cases not much above the savage, ignorant, of a slow sensibility, unstimulated by the arts and luxuries of civilization. Their passions have not yet much refined above the elemental. For that fine and ennobling love which is the fruit of advanced culture they have not yet developed the capacity. But the maternal instinct remains among them in all its primitive strength. And it has not to divide its sovereignty with the emotions of a later culture. Relatively its force is greater, because undivided.

But, it must be said, in no class does maternal affection arouse, as it should, that persistent and laborious effort to tend and educate, which is its worthiest criterion. The Indian mother is lavish with her caresses and endearments, as in other moods she may fly into fits of uncontrolled anger. But, except for the lengthy period of nursing, sometimes three and ordinarily two years, to which she is willing to devote herself, she shows only too little of that continuous and intelligent care which is expected from a mother. Largely no doubt this is due to ignorance. She has not—one might with justice say she is not allowed to have—the knowledge which is needed to be a good mother. She is unaware of the most elementary requirements of sanitation and health. Worse still, she has not been trained to know the importance of compelling good habits and regular discipline in early childhood. Again, though she is usually an affectionate, she is not often an inspiring, mother. She is probably at her best as she sees her children fed with the food she has cooked herself, giving to each the tit-bits that she can, looking lovingly to their comforts, herself waiting till all are done before she sits down to her own meal. This is the memory that lingers most closely in the Indian's mind as the man grows older and leans on retrospect. To most European children the remembrance that is dearest is that of his mother stooping over his cot to kiss him good-night, radiant in beauty, clad in silks and laces, with the gleam of white shoulders and precious stones to set off the soft curves of her dear face, before she leaves for a dinner, a theatre, or a ball. He is proud of her looks, so transformed, and of her charm, proud that he belongs to a being so splendid and so wonderful. But to the Indian the picture that recurs is of ungrudging kindly service. And perhaps the prolonged nursing period, bad as in other respects it is—bad especially for the over-taxed mother—serves to draw closer the bond between her and the child, already conscious of its own existence. Certain it is that the Indian son, as he grows up, forbears ever to judge his mother. Of Indian women generally, or of the mothers of other men, he may complain for their ignorance and their disregard of matters which he has taught himself to consider necessary; he may even with some unfairness blame them for a want of steadfast purpose and regularity, which is by no means peculiar to their sex. But for his own mother he preserves a constant respect and loving solicitude.

Yet, all said and done, it is not in motherhood, but rather in her love, that the Indian woman has reached her highest achievement. The devotion and self-sacrifice which are hers form a triumph of the spirit;

IN THE HAPPY VALLEY OF KASHMIR

and she clothes these virtues with sensuous charm and transcendent ecstasy. She gives freely of herself with both hands, by service and surrender, by wistfulness and delight.

It is in the quality of social charm that the Indian woman is most often lacking. For the man she loves she can command every grace. She can be coaxing, caressing, kind, gentle, tender, submissive, all in one. Even to the stranger, alone in her family as guest or dependent, she shows herself solicitous and kindly, with a pleasing quiet charm that comes from the heart. But she has not the habit of social entertainment or that special training, so much a matter of a quickened intelligence, which is required to set general acquaintances at ease or to lead a conversation which should be at once comprehensive and light. She has no general coquetry and is often without that ease of manner and unconstrained grace of movement in a crowded room, which can hardly be acquired otherwise than by the habitual usage of good society. This lapse from complete achievement marks itself most strongly in the intonations of her voice. For it must, alack, be admitted that the Indian woman's voice is her weak point. Here are few of those soft, round, low but clear mezzos and contraltos which like bronze bells sound so deliciously in a European drawing-room. The voice in India seems seldom to have that steady control and rounded *timbre* which is gained from the repression of strained and uneven notes and the modulation of all tones to one easy key. The

Indian girl is not even taught to sing and knows nothing of voice production. What little she does sing, untaught or worse than untaught, is more often a scream than a real melody. Good voices are almost the monopoly of the professional dancing girl. Hence even in ordinary conversation, a lady's speech tends to harsh and abrupt sounds, shrill and not beautiful. Her intonation is only too often an antidote to the charms of her fastidious neatness and her kindly eyes and smile.

Society, it must be said, and social converse had in India ceased to exist some fifteen hundred years ago. It does not happen that a company of men and women meet on easy terms for entertainment with the pleasures of light and familiar conversation, not learned, never, please heaven, didactic or instructive, but clever, witty, illumined by intuitions and swift generalizations, light of touch, and near to laughter. Nor is anything known of that innocent coquetry of well-bred womanhood, which seeks no particular stimulations but appeals for a general admiration, impersonally given to that fine spirited, finely attractive being who is the last word in luxury and taste and womanly moderation.

In India as one knows it—whatever it may have been in the remoter age pictured in the caves of Ajanta—the aspirations of women have taken a different course through a more placid water. Where they steer is no ebb and flow of conflicting purpose and sometimes, as they pass listlessly to the shore, it looks almost as if the roadstead had come to a stagnation. And yet—yet the course is set correctly and the sun is rightly taken. It may be that the horizon is viewed too low and that the profundities of the human spirit are not yet plumbed; but the Indian woman crosses the waters of life on a line true to her nature and her functions.

There is in all the Indian languages which derive from Sanscrit a word whose habitual usage is significant of a whole attitude to life, by whose meaning alone it is possible to understand the position sought by and accorded to womanhood. It is the word "*dharma*," which has been constantly mistranslated into English as "religion." But when an Indian speaks of "*dharma*" he means really the duties, divinely imposed if you like or valid in nature, of his station. Between this "*dharma*" and that, between the "*dharma*" of his own class or sex and that of others, he draws a sharp distinction. In England, too, this sense is not unknown and the great landlord, for instance, speaks with right of the duties of his position, contrasting them with a broad distinction to those of the merchant, for example, or the workman. *Noblesse oblige* is a proverb that has been applied in all countries. But throughout Western thought there runs the idea that duty and morals must at bottom be one and the same for all. It is only, one might say, as a concession that the special duties of each station are recognized; and at most they are referred rather to the accidentals of life, to those supererogatory virtues which may be expected, like magnanimity or liberality from the rich and powerful, or that exceptional patience and humility which many persons seem to expect from the needy and unfortunate. The basic more permanent rules of moral conduct are regarded as something absolute, unalterable, unconditioned. Even the differences of sex are forgotten in the abstract contemplation of fixed moral laws. In practice, of course, facts have often compelled peoples to admit that differences do exist in the application of rules of conduct. Thus, to take a recent instance, in the crisis of war public opinion has allowed that even the supreme duties of citizenship press with divergent force upon married and unmarried men. Similarly it was until recently recognized by all and is even now by the greatest number that there are matters in which the conduct of men and women cannot be the same and that the same rights and duties cannot be applied indiscriminately to both sexes. But the recognition was seldom more than tacit. It was never co-ordinated, at least in England, to a reasoned view of life. It was not built upon a deliberate analysis of natural differences in function and in sensory and nervous force. It tended rather to be a mere concession to passing conditions of life. Thought, when it was explicit, dwelt chiefly upon abstract ideas of equality and equal duties. Some writers even tried to explain away the differences of character between men and women by referring them to mere accidents of environment, to women getting a less thorough education, for

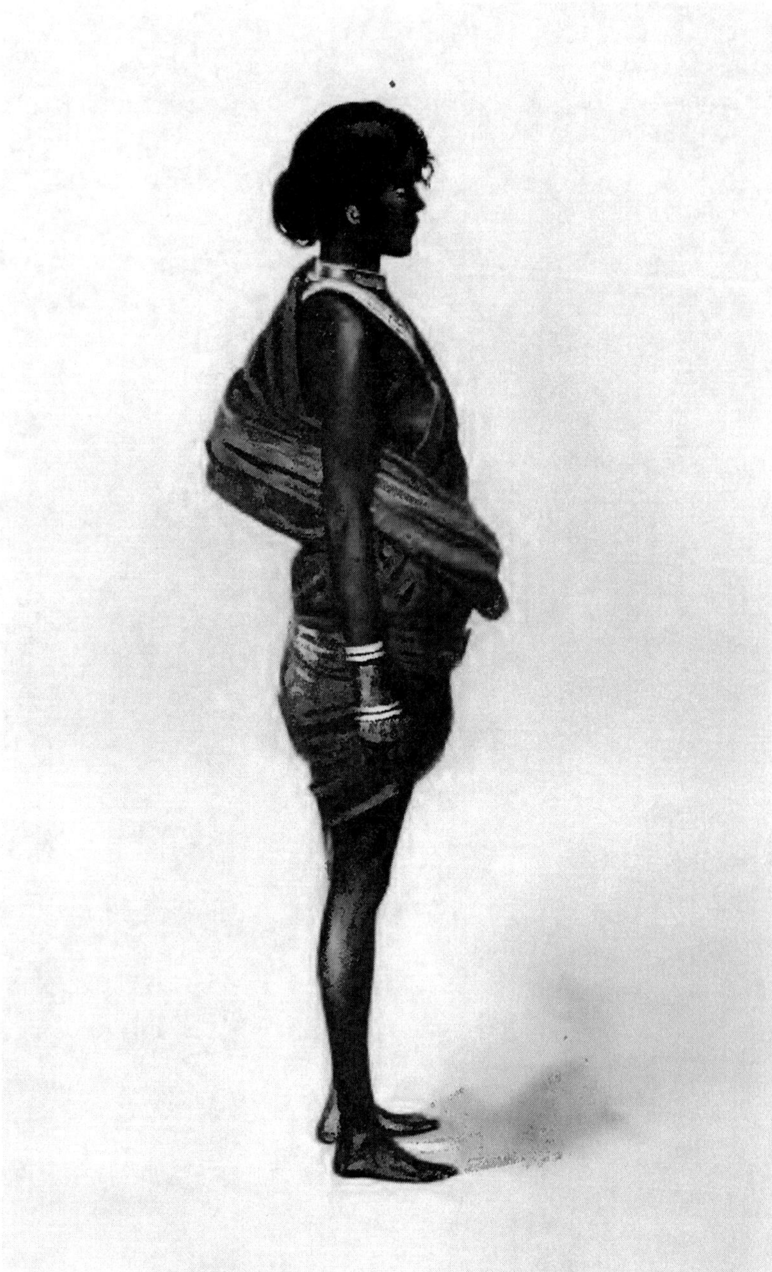

A DENIZEN OF THE WESTERN GHAUTS

instance, or less of a chance in life, as it was called. It was not openly and clearly recognized that the natures and functions of men and women were different in essentials, and that the rules of conduct must in consequence be relative to different needs and purposes.

In India, the way in which "*dharma*" is understood has made such a mistake impossible. From its implications it is believed by all, or has until the last few years been believed, that duty must necessarily be relative to function and must correspond with fitness to inner nature. A distinction so obvious and primary as that of sex can in consequence be ignored by none except a few recent abstract thinkers. The rights and duties of women are defined in relation to the activities which are imposed on them by the principles of their nature; and the ideal which is painted is in harmony with the natural laws of flesh and spirit. Modesty, self-sacrifice, tenderness, neatness, all that is delicate and fastidious, those are qualities which have a natural propriety. To play her modest part in the family household quietly, to sweeten life within the radius of her influence, to serve her children, to please the man to whom she is dedicated, to receive pleasure in her love, and find happiness in the pleasures that she gives, that is a woman's "*dharma*"—her fitting performance of function. It is not, of course, that Hinduism does not know that men and women are alike in respect of certain faculties and both alike distinguished from other living creatures. But it has laid more stress upon the differences in function. It has been able to see that the being of each separate man and woman is one and indivisible, and that sex is not a mere distinction added or subtracted but rather the shape in which the whole living, acting human creature is cast and moulded. This, which is the teaching of India's philosophies, is also the practical wisdom of her peoples. And this it is which has kept Indian women so superbly natural, so calmly insistent on their sex. In Northern Europe, it may perhaps be said, the evolution of womanhood has more rapidly progressed, in response to a quickly developing environment ; but in as far as it has rejected nature and inner law, it may the rather tend to be in fact a *devolution*, a turn or twist *from* the road and not a progress. In India evolution has been slow, cramped by unnecessary superstitions and arbitrary abstentions, but in its main lines at least it is consistent and natural. Its form is not unsuitable ; though it still has to be filled with a larger and richer content.

But the content of life in India is in truth already being enriched. Her women are no mere abstractions, fixed and immovable, to be delineated by thin conventional lines. Rather must they be thought of as a mass of concrete, distinguishable, living human beings, moving as a whole towards a larger freedom. Only a century ago when the greatest of German thinkers, Hegel, wrote his "Philosophy of History" he could with no little truth say that "Indian culture had not attained to a recognition of freedom and inner morality," and could assert that in the Indian soul there was "bound up an irrational imagination which attaches the moral value and character of men to an infinity of outward actions as empty in point of intellect as of feeling, and sets aside all respect for the welfare of men and even makes a duty of the cruellest and severest contravention of it." Women of course in all countries are far more conservative than men and are more readily content to sink the needs of personality in a general level of unruffled action. Yet even among the women of India a new spirit of liberation from external limitations is becoming visible and an aspiration to an excellence that shall be from within. In spite of caste distinctions, in spite of the forced rigidity of the marriage system, in spite of all the mental unrest and error of the educated and the practical inertia of the unread, in spite of all this and much more, it would now be far from true to say of them as a whole that they are unconscious of inward freedom and inward law or are blind to the needs of human welfare in the conditions of human life.

But this inner freedom and external amplitude need not be sought and will not be gained in the imitation of foreign manners and customs. Such imitation can never be anything but unnatural and inharmonious; and the castes which have tried it have not succeeded in avoiding evil consequences. A better way is to revert to the ancient ideals which still inspire all that is good in later practice. Dark ages of ignorance have pruned and pinched the older, freer spirit, by superstitious and absurd asceticisms and misinterpreted authorities. Only the ruling castes have enlarged themselves from the bondage by their more virile audacities. In general even the primitive and natural classes, as they raise their status and become reflective, succumb to the same narrowing limitations and impose upon their womankind disabilities which are external and mechanical but which they see current in the higher Brahmanized classes. Yet in the older, nobler days, the Indian women had a life larger by far and more rich in fulfilment. To regain this, which after all is still a living ideal, and to ennoble and enlarge it further through that Greek thought—that inspiring humanity and breath of happiness—which is the life-giving element of European science and civilization, that were indeed an end worthy of a fine tradition. To cut away from the bonds of fears and artificialities and non-human hopes and terrors and seek only to *be*, wholly and fully, in the harmony of nature and function and sane development, preserving the eternal virtues of womanhood, and finely conscious of a proud tradition—by some such purpose surely might it be possible to secure safe continuity and social health while attaining a progressive and extended activity that should not be alien or discordant. But the timidities of crude asceticism must first be overcome. A generation must arise which can comprehend that self-control is not abstention, far from it, but is found only when a

A WORKING WOMAN AT AJMERE

free soul, governing itself by its own laws, seeks its own satisfaction and the development of all its functions in its free activities. To deny human nature, for any price however fanciful, is more harmful by far than the "Fay ce que Voudras" of any Abbaye de Thelème.

Of the narrow and incongruous privations with which the old ideals were overlaid in the later decadence many still remain. Most cruel and least defensible of all is the prejudice, common in all classes except the highest and not unknown even there, against the enjoyment of literature and art. Music is discountenanced, pictures are never seen, even reading and writing is thought unwomanly. When not only the charming likeness drawn of women in old books is remembered, but in actual life also one sees the fine harmony achieved by those ladies, Rájputs perhaps or Nágar Brahmans, who can recite and enjoy poetry and even sing or play instruments—with what far greater happiness to themselves and the men they love!—it should be plain how great is the national loss wrought by this empty deprivation. Of all the European countries, it is in France that women have most nearly attained that final excellence which both accords with the true tradition of Western life and is not out of harmony with their nature. There a sane and wise worldliness has led to an incessant regard to neatness and careful management, an avoidance of all that is wasteful or excessive. And French life of course pivots upon a mixed society, easily mingling in graceful and polished intercourse—an urbane fellowship in a human *civitas*, a citizenship in whose enjoyment, it might almost seem, lies the last test of civilization. Hence the French woman, for her part, has trained herself or been trained to be the instrument of a symphony of urbanity and well-bred fellowship, giving of her own characteristic qualities to be an inspiration and a standard to the creative art. Yet, with it all, she is emphatic of her sex. From the highest to the lowest class, one may see her, neat, well dressed, choice in adornment, lavish of love. But she is also tirelessly ready to serve, in her house-keeping as in affairs, devoted to the family of which she is the living bond, an affectionate but careful mother who is honoured and loved by her sons with a pure and tender fervour. For in France, in spite of the general European tendency to moral absolutes at least in theory, the balanced sanity and practical wisdom of the people has never failed to recognize the different spheres and powers, qualities and weaknesses, of men and women. And further, Greek thought and an unbroken Roman tradition have kept alive in France the ideal of a temperate and steady fruition of a world that is made for mankind. In India conditions are different and there is no tradition of mixed society with an easy untrammelled exchange of ideas. Yet even within the limits of the family, it might be thought, the added enjoyment and the larger and finer interests that would be gained by some such acquaintance with books and music and paintings, and the nobler emotions thus won, should seem desirable to all who can think at all.

Controversy has raged fiercely in India round this question of woman's education. The number of women who can even read and write, if all classes in the whole country are regarded, is a negligible quantity, so small it is; and there are vast tracts in which even Brahman girls remain wholly illiterate. There are many to this day who bitterly oppose even the teaching of letters to girl-children. That this can be the case is of course due to the ignorance of their parents. They have not yet been able to grasp, nor do they know their own ancient history to sufficient purpose, that reading and writing is the birth-right of every human being and a necessary condition of all intelligence and rational development. They are not aware that the ancient ideal contemplated no such renouncement. And quite without cause they fear that instruction for a few years in the elements of education would interfere with the routine of family life and the customs of marriage. They have perhaps never had it clearly put to them how simply this instruction could be fitted in with the usual programme of an ordinary household and how it need imply no departure from existing practice in other matters. But indefensible though this opposition to elementary instruction must be, the objections against further education are unfortunately by no means without excuse. For it must with bitterness be confessed that the modern world, at any rate in Europe, has not yet devised any suitable system of higher education for girls, has indeed rather busied itself with what is unsuitable and injurious. "Advanced thinkers" and "social leaders" have a way of shutting their eyes to scientific results; and facts are hard things which a flabby age prefers to ignore. So girls have been encouraged to emulate boys and young men in every sort of examination within the same curriculum, without heed of their earlier precocity, different method of nervous activity and smaller reserve force, to the detriment of health and natural talents and to their unfitting for their own purposes and functions. It is this which Indian parents, with an eye open to facts when they are so broad and natural as the facts of sex, have apprehended, however dimly, and as it were unconsciously. They have guessed what higher education must in all probability mean in India, as long as European education remained unchanged. And they would not let their girls run the risk of an education which might distort, rather than develop, their sex. Late events served further to deepen this strong and instinctive distrust; and it is indisputable that the excesses of an unhappy section of English women with abnormal aspirations have set back the cause of women's education in India by many decades.

The misfortune is that in India opposition does not confine itself to a particular and, one hopes, a temporary phase of secondary education; nor does it recognize that in all countries, and especially in India with its universal and early marriage, the question of

BORN BESIDE THE SACRED RIVERS

higher education can affect only a very small number of the total. The feeling of dislike is instinctive and intuitional rather than a reasoned criticism, and it has crept on like a cloud of smoke over the whole field of elementary education. Necessarily it has also obscured all view of a possible, better indigenous method of higher education, which should at once be consonant with the traditions of ancient India and the needs of women in Indian society. Such a system appears now to have been set under way in the wonder-working country of Japan, and with little change might probably be made suitable to Indian conditions. It deserves at least to be studied without prejudice and with a settled understanding of the requirements of the land and of the small classes of women who would directly benefit.

In spite of all obstacles, due partly to the decay of older customs, partly also to imported confusions, it may be hoped that before long it will be admitted that every girl must be taught to read and write. And one may even hope that a higher education will ensue which, without slurring over a woman's earlier precocity and special talents, without ignoring her specific duties as wife and mother, without forgetting the peculiar needs and excellences of her mind and body, will in addition make her more liberal, better instructed, a worthier companion and a nobler inspiration. In India happily a girl is already allowed to know the facts of life and her emotions are at least natural. But such an education as one foresees would teach her to know more clearly and with scientific truth how to be at once a pleasing and happy wife and a good mother. She, and through her the children whom she trains, would learn the evils of premature or too constantly recurring child-birth and how to avoid them easily. She would know also how to protect her family from uncleanly surroundings and unwholesome habits. She would not unlearn but rather be taught even better the necessary arts of cooking and of sewing, the latter nowadays in many cases almost unknown. But in addition she would also learn to appreciate the beauties of language and of craftsmanship, to hear and understand great poetry, and to feel her whole being thrill to a more glorious harmony in response to the call of the fine arts. She would still—like the Nair ladies of whom old Duarte Barbosa wrote—"hold it a great honour to please men." Yet she would please not merely by her passion and purity and service, but, keeping these, would also create a higher attraction of the spirit. Thus would the lotus women of India be in truth such that of each it might be said: "She walks delicately like a swan and her voice is low and musical as the note of the cuckoo, calling softly in the summer day. . . . She is gracious and clever, pious and respectful, a lover of God, a listener to the virtuous and the wise."

"It may be all my love went wrong—
A scribe's work writ awry and blurred,
Scrawled after the blind evensong—
Spoilt music with no perfect word."

The Leper. SWINBURNE.

Published by

Facsimile Publisher
Ashok Vihar, Delhi-110052 (India)
Website: www.facsimilepublisher.com

Distributed by

Gyan Books Pvt. Ltd.
5, Ansari Road, Daryaganj, New Delhi-110002 (India)
E-mail: books@gyanbooks.com, Website: www.gyanbooks.com

2 222000 015350